ALLAN

BIG OP!.

MAD LOVE.

ONE!

MICHAEL JOSEPH

Published by the Penguin Group
Penguin Books Ltd, 80 Strand, London WC2R 0RL, England
Penguin Group (USA) Inc., 375 Hudson Street, New York, New York 10014, USA
Penguin Group (Canada), 90 Eglinton Avenue East, Suite 700, Toronto, Ontario,
Canada M4P 2Y3 (a division of Pearson Penguin Canada Inc.)
Penguin Ireland, 25 St Stephen's Green, Dublin 2, Ireland
(a division of Penguin Books Ltd)
Penguin Group (Australia), 250 Camberwell Road,
Camberwell, Victoria 3124, Australia (a division of Pearson Australia Group Pty Ltd)
Penguin Books India Pvt Ltd, 11 Community Centre,
Panchsheel Park, New Delhi – 110 017, India
Penguin Group (NZ), cnr Airborne and Rosedale Roads, Albany,
Auckland 1310, New Zealand (a division of Pearson New Zealand Ltd)
Penguin Books (South Africa) (Pty) Ltd, 24 Sturdee Avenue,
Rosebank, Johannesburg 2196, South Africa

Penguin Books Ltd, Registered Offices: 80 Strand, London WC2 0RL England

www.penguin.com

First published 2006
1

Copyright © 2006 MTVN MTV.Com, MTV: Music Television, PIMP MY RIDE and all related
titles and logos are trademarks of MTV Networks, A Division of Viacom
International Inc.

The moral right of the author has been asserted

Produced for Michael Joseph by Essential Works, 168a Camden Street, London NW1 9PT

Printed in Great Britain by Butler & Tanner Ltd, Frome, Somerset

A CIP catalogue record for this book is available from the British Library

ISBN-13: 978–0–718–14974–1
ISBN-10: 0–718–14974–2

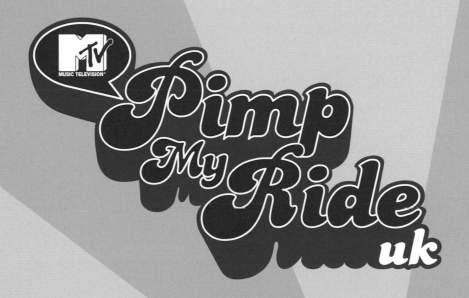

Michael Joseph
an imprint of
PENGUIN BOOKS

# Contents

# Introduction

## by Tim Westwood

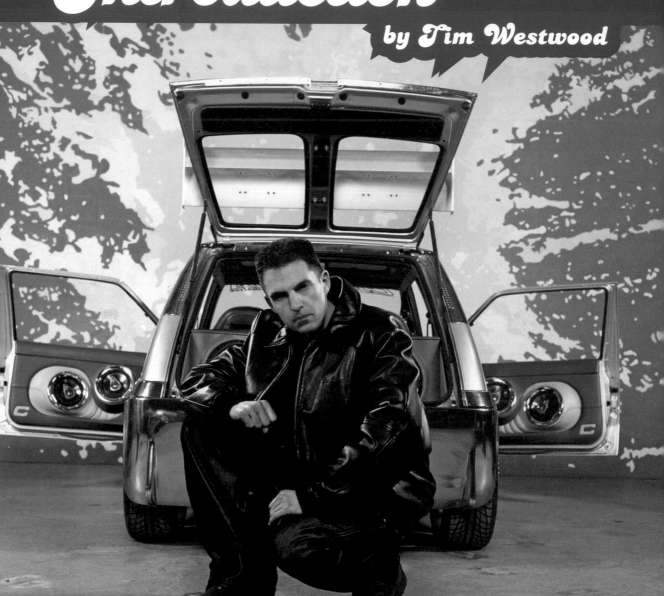

When I knock on somebody's door and say "I'm here to pimp your ride – UK style," the look on their face makes me feel like Father Christmas. I'm blessing them with a gift that will change their life forever!

And when the cover is pulled off to reveal their pimped-out ride people go wild, hyperventilate, cry, faint, and jump up and down.

An incredible paint job, massive chrome rims, all new interiors, TVs and maxed-out sound systems all come as standard. It's all about that fantasy pimpin' that makes no sense – a skate ramp on a Panda, a beach in a Sunny and an electronic basketball scoreboard in a Capri.

'Pimpin' now means extreme, blingtastic, mad-over-the-top – a celebration of car customisation. The car may be worth £40 but we spend 40 grand!

Cars have been part of the hip-hop game for many years. I love rocking big American trucks sitting on chrome shoes the size of fat ladies' waistlines. Tricked out with creative non-factory modification that makes your joint look blazin' hot. And it's an international franchise it's only right the UK should represent.

Since I've been holding down Pimp My Ride UK, there is one question everyone asks, no matter where I am – in a supermarket doing my shopping, in a restaurant getting my eat on, or even when I'm in the gents standing at the porcelain. Nowadays when I'm DJing people don't request records they ask me to pimp their ride. It's changed my world – now parents relate to me through their young kids, and grannies love me. Bless.

Tim Westwood

# Morris Minor

# Please MTV, Pimp My Ride

## Pimpee... Bethan Jones

Twenty-five-year-old Bethan bought her Morris Minor off eBay for £500 in the summer of 2004. She knew as soon as she saw it in the flesh that it was a wreck – but she fell in love with it, anyway. "The advert said it needed a bit of TLC to get it up and running and looking pretty," she says. "But I hadn't quite bargained for exactly how much TLC."

Bethan feels nostalgic towards Morris Minors: her mum and dad had one when they first got married. She thought it could be a dream wedding car for her and her boyfriend, John. Her wedding dream was completed by the idea of taking the Minor on a surfing honeymoon to Cornwall. "I absolutely love surfing," she says. "But at the moment there's nowhere to put the boards. And the state it's in, I doubt it would even make it two blocks down the road, never mind to the beach."

Bethan's wedding/honeymoon dream seems a world away at the moment: her ride is rusty, smelly, it rattles, and is freezing cold, and when it rains she has to pull over because the windscreen wipers go too slow. The wing-mirrors rattle and Bethan has to rely on her passengers to be lookouts – when she *has* any passengers: "At the moment, my mates are embarrassed to be seen in the car and my mum refuses to even ride in it. If MTV doesn't rescue my ride, I can't imagine I'm going to get married, I'm going to end up an old spinster..."

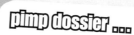

## pimp dossier ...

- » **Name:** Bethan Jones
- » **Ride:** Morris Minor (1961)
- » **Lives:** Enfield, Middlesex
- » **Daytime:** photography student
- » **Loves:** photography, surfing, indie/rock
- » **Is:** bubbly, sincere, down-to-earth, good fun
- » **Wants:** a car to get married in
- » **Not expecting:** a back-to-the-factory restoration – up for something funky!

## Westwood's verdict

Bethan's Morris Minor is nothing but a banger. When it rolled off the production line in 1961, JFK was president and Elvis was No 1: they're long dead and buried and Bethan's car looks like it should have joined them. It does not feel good at all: what's up with all those felt-tip circles on the paintwork? Where's the radio? Where's the heater? What's the 'start' button? It's a straight mess. My *mum* used to have those flip-out indicators. Bethan wants to take it to Cornwall? That's not going to happen. This car's straight busted. Scrap. It will *never* make the beach. Bethan's car game is weak – but we're going to fix it.

 Bethan – you ARE going to get married. Holla! **westwood**

# Pimp Plan...

" Some people choose to restore their Morris Minors to the way they first looked when they came out of the factory. We decided to give Bethan a totally modern classic; to take it out of the past, and not only update it – but take it right into the future. " **jamie**

" We're going to make a little space in the boot for all Bethan's surf gear and make a little seat where Bethan and her new hubby can chill out and watch the sunset go down... "
martin

" I'm going to lower the suspension, get it looking sweet, getting rid of these nasty old 'steelies'. " **junior**

"This has got to be Bethan's wedding car – the most important day of her life. If you're not letting me do anything weddingy on the outside, I need to do something weddingy on the inside. Real leather interior, a wedding theme, very girly... **pinky**

"Bethan's well into her photography, so I'm thinking a mobile studio, so wherever she goes she can pursue her passion. It's not easy fitting everything into a car of this size. I'm thinking a top-of-the-range mini-digital camera, a printer in the glove box and a laptop in the back, so she can send images from anywhere in the world. **bluey**

"Paint-wise, we're going to get away from the classic restoration job and get more into the surf scene. Maybe with a touch of the hot-rod scene. Flames running down the side. That'll be excellent. **ronnie**

# Pimping It

One of the best things we did with the Minor was the laptop: we had to rebuild the whole console to fit it. Obviously, a Minor doesn't have a 21st-century console so we built a whole structure so that you could sit in the back and work on a laptop. That took a couple of days but it turned out pretty cool. And the paint job was one of the best ones of the series, too.

## Exterior

- Chrome replaced
- Replacement rear silencer with chrome outlet
- Custom tail-pipe
- Retro roof rack
- Lowered suspension
- Clifford Intellistart alarm with water-jet warning squirters

" When we first started stripping back the doors, we found that two of them were totally rotten – that was an extra job we hadn't bargained on: we had to get hold of two replacement doors and do a lot of work on them to make them fit. " **martin**

# Interior

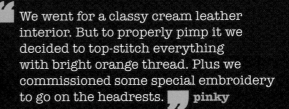

We went for a classy cream leather interior. But to properly pimp it we decided to top-stitch everything with bright orange thread. Plus we commissioned some special embroidery to go on the headrests. **pinky**

- Replacement headlining with orange neoprene from Snugg

- Fabricated centre console with (retro-style) Pioneer head unit DEH-P77MP

- Photo-storage compartment

- Re-trimmed leather Simoni Racing steering wheel X2350LYX

- Chrome gear knob 532200, hand brake lever
- FX7111GR, chrome pedal set 880PX all Simoni Racing from Auto Inparts

- Headrests with Mrs (driver) & Mr (passenger) orange embroidered logos

## Paint

● Re-sprayed in vibrant Tangerine Kandy from House of Kolor

● Striped, hot-rod design in contrasting yellow with silver border

" Until now, Bethan hadn't even had a radio in her car. It was so loud it would have been pointless – you wouldn't have heard the sound over the engine. Step one to solving this? Apply soundproofing to the whole car. Then we fitted a CD head unit to a 6-disc CD changer, with speakers in every door, all powered by two huge amps in the boot. " **bluey**

" To get the Minor looking really hot took time: eight coats of paint and a total of two weeks from start to finish. We applied primer, then two layers of a silver base coat. Then, after five layers of Tangerine Kandy, it looked pretty much ready to set the road on fire. " **ronnie**

# Ice

- 12in Apple iBook with D-Link Bluetooth adaptor DBT-120
- Canon compact CP-330 printer
- 7.2 mega pixel Powershot S70 Canon camera with waterproof case
- Orange Nokia 6630 mobile phone with Bluetooth
- 2 'Pimped' Quiksilver surfboards with wetsuits to match
- Coga PA multi-sound horn to play the 'Wedding March'
- 6-disc CD changer Pioneer CDX-P670

# Wheels

- 7.5 × 18in Matrix from Wolfrace with Toyo Proxos 215/35/18 tyres all round

# Morris Minor
## Pimped

When I dumped Bethan's
Morris Minor at the Garage,
it was straight busted.
But the boys have flipped
the script. Now the joint's
straight blazing. It's off the
meter! **westwood**

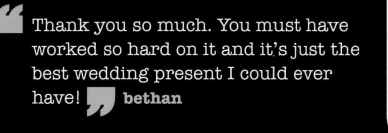

"Thank you so much. You must have worked so hard on it and it's just the best wedding present I could ever have! **bethan**

# The Team

The guys at the garage are gonna bless your ride with the mad flava. Holla! **westwood**

**Martin**

Bodywork

**Bluey**

Audio & Multimedia

**Ronnie**

Paintwork

**Matty**

Crew

**Pinky**

Design

**Richie**

Accessories

**Junior**

Wheels & Tyres

**Steve**

Crew

**Jamie**

The Boss

**In action**

**Westwood**

Big Dawg

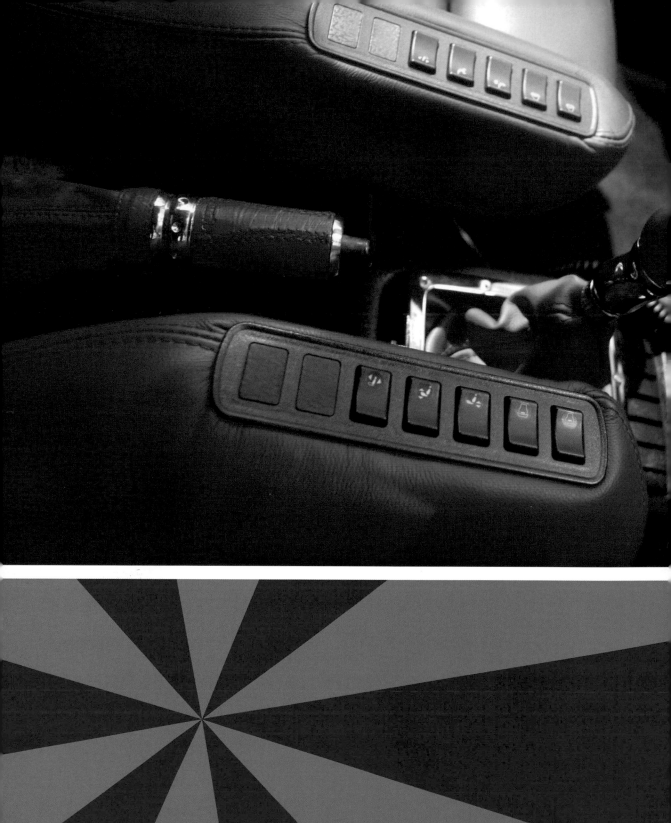

VW Golf

# Please MTV, Pimp My Ride

**Pimpee... Asif Nawab**

Nineteen-year-old Asif says he eats, sleeps and drinks football. He supports Arsenal and used to play left-back for a Sunday side until injuries forced him to stop. Now, he spends his spare time coaching junior teams at his club, Flamengo Juniors in Leyton, East London. "Football is my life," he says.

His 1989 VW Golf is the nervecentre of his football management. Asif uses it to ferry kit and equipment to training sessions. Asif's coaching is not just about football: he wants to show the kids the right way to live, too: "I want to teach them that hard work and staying on the straight and narrow will get you rewards," he says. "You don't have to be the tough, bling-bling man to get through life."

Asif also does a bit of work on his Golf. But that's not such good work. "I give myself 10 out of 10 for effort," he says. "But the car is still a shambles." That's being kind. What's wrong with his car? What's right with it? The mirrors are broken and keep dropping off; the hand-me-down stereo doesn't fit (it's held in with *coins)*; you can hear Asif coming from miles away as the Golf squeaks and creaks round the back streets. Even his *Gran* thinks the car's shabby. "The car is such an embarrassment," says Asif. "All my mates laugh at me for driving it."

What can the boys at the garage do for him?

## pimp dossier ▪▪▪

- » **Name:** Asif Nawab
- » **Ride:** 1989 VW Golf Mark II
- » **Lives:** Chingford, Essex
- » **Daytime:** software engineering student
- » **Loves:** football, r'n'b, hip hop
- » **Is:** nice guy who helps out his gran and tries to show local kids right way to live
- » **Wants:** his ride pimped to help him with his voluntary work with the Flamengo Juniors 4-16s sides

## Westwood's verdict...

Don't get me wrong – a Golf Mark II can be a hot ride. But Asif's isn't even lukewarm. If he's serious about being a player, things really need to change. He's had a go at some improvements himself but it's not happening: I don't know about 'do-it-yourself': it looks more like destroy-it-yourself. He'll never win any championships with this car. It's all busted. His rust game is intense. This is just scrap here. It's a bad look. We've got one choice: dump it or pimp it!

" Asif may be a defender on the football pitch – but how does he defend THIS? It's an own goal. " **westwood**

# Pimp Plan...

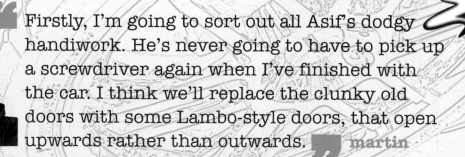

❝Asif's Golf is not in the best condition – and neither is Asif. We know that a couple of years ago, he got ill and had to give up playing football. Footballers' cars these days have got so much bling-bling: we need to give Asif's car some serious respect on the pitch and on the streets. ❞ **jamie**

❝Asif's been feeling blue about his Golf for too long – we're going to give him the baddest blackest Mark II on the block. ❞
**ronnie**

❝Firstly, I'm going to sort out all Asif's dodgy handiwork. He's never going to have to pick up a screwdriver again when I've finished with the car. I think we'll replace the clunky old doors with some Lambo-style doors, that open upwards rather than outwards. ❞ **martin**

"Asif's had a really hard time the last couple of years. He deserves a really nice and classy leather interior: I'm thinking red – not only because it will look and feel good, but it will also show off his love for Arsenal. **pinky**

"Asif was really worried about his car getting stolen – even before we started pimping it. Well, fresh off the production line, I've got one of the best alarm systems you've ever seen: the car will actually TEXT Asif to let him know if a thief is trying to break in! **jamie**

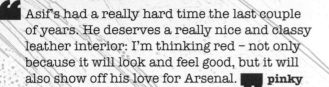

"We'll be ripping out Asif's beat-up old radio and replacing it with a brand new multi-CD and DVD system along with a games console loaded with the latest football games. Asif will be able to sit in the back seat and watch screens laid into the head-rests of the seats in front of him. **bluey**

"The bigger the wheels, the cooler the car. I'm going to widen the arches and make way for some big rims: some phat 18-inch chromes will make him look like a serious player. **junior**

# Pimping It

Jamie came up with the Lambo door idea for this – they were first seen on the Lamborghini Countach, which came out in 1974. There are lots of little things we put on the cars that you don't see on the TV show: on the Golf, we put a little electric rotating buffer on the back so Asif could get the mud off his football boots!

## Exterior

- Big bumper kit added
- Lexus lights to rear
- DTM-style wing-mirrors
- Replacement rear stainless steel silencer with DTM back box
- Lamborghini-style door conversion kit from LSD
- Smoke-tinted windows
- Customised boot-cleaner concealed under the back bumper

" We pimped the bumpers, the lights, the mirrors... everything we could get our hands on – and we added the ultimate celebrity touch: smoke-tinted windows " **martin**

# Interior

"Because of Asif's injury, we need to do something extra special. We put in some heated electric seats, built for people with sports injuries: they've been especially designed to give you perfect posture and they cost a mere... £1200 each. We also installed a full in-seat heating and massage system into the seats. **pinky**

- Red auto leather from Yarwood throughout

- Front and rear door panels re-fabricated/ leather trimmed with angular (retro-style) speaker builds housing Pioneer TS-C1700R component speakers (Mid/tweeter)

- Replacement front seats; Recaro Ergomeds, trimmed leather

- Heated 8-point massage pads built into the two front seats with remote controls

## Paint

- Re-sprayed in metallic black from House of Kolor with red sparkle flakes
- Striped graphics across the bonnet
- "ASIF 3" on the top of the roof in vinyl graphic, as numbers on the back of a football shirt

## Ice

" We built Asif a hi-tech coaching zone in the boot of his Golf. On his parcel shelf, we made room for a 15-inch LCD flip-up screen. Finally, we put in a tactics board to slide out of the boot, so Asif can show his players what he wants them to do. We added a sound system including two 1000-watt sub-woofers, run from two fully digital amplifiers. There was also a fridge in each door and, back in the boot, a storage area filled with all-new football equipment. " **bluey**

" First, we applied primer, then we gave it three layers of stealth black paint. We also threw in some extra sparkle – so that when the car catches the sun, you're gonna need to wear shades. Finally, we put a big "Asif 3" on the roof. " ronnie

- Pioneer head unit X1
- 15.2in flip up (we spun the flip down!) Centurion RE-1569 screen
- 2 × Centurion FD6569 6.5in screen monitors fitted in the headrests
- Component speaker sets ACIS63 from Audiobahn
- 2 × 10in Audiobahn Subwoofers AW1000N mounted in the boot
- Also in the boot 2 × A1504DP Amplifiers from Audiobahn
- AVSW4Q Audio/video selector
- Viper alarm which texts your mobile phone if it's broken into!

## Wheels

- 7.5 × 18in Cataluyna Chrome from TSW with Yokohama 215/35/18 tyres all round

# VW Golf Pimped

"When I drove the Golf into the garage, it was a terrible look. It was straight disrespectful. It didn't feel good. But the boys have blessed it with the mad flava." **westwood**

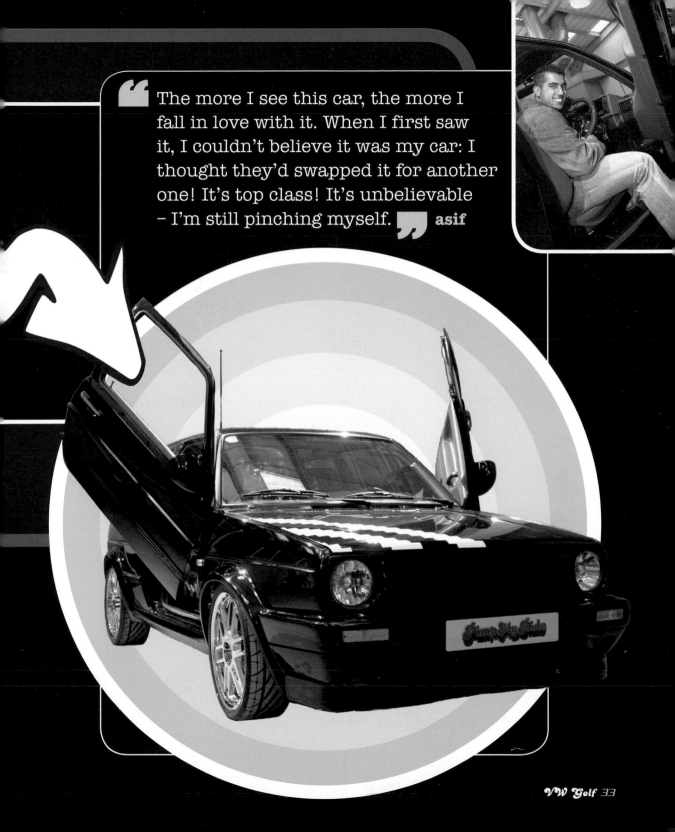

The more I see this car, the more I fall in love with it. When I first saw it, I couldn't believe it was my car: I thought they'd swapped it for another one! It's top class! It's unbelievable – I'm still pinching myself. **asif**

# Jamie "The Boss"

" I'm a big crispy duck and pancakes man. "

How many cars have you got?
Four.

What do you ask for when you have your hair cut?
I don't. I take in a drawing.

What are you thinking of when you do the drawing?
I'm the most symmetrical person in the world, apart from when it comes to my hair.

Favourite bit of clothing?
Clothes that I've made myself, because no-one else has got it. Jeans – people ask, 'Where did you get them from?' It's just the self-contentment of making things myself.

Favourite TV show?
Grand Designs: I love that programme. I love houses.

Favourite film?
The Serpent and The Rainbow – based on a true story about Voodoo in Haiti. Very scary, because it's true. Terrifying.

Favourite takeaway?
Chinese. I'm a big crispy duck and pancakes man. I could eat a whole duck quite easily. Duck for one, please.

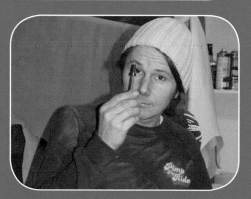

# Ford Granada Hearse

## Westwood's verdict

This is not my car of choice. I wouldn't want this to be my last ride. In fact, I'd rather go by bus to my own funeral. I wouldn't even bury my dog in this. A hearse is a classic car – but this is a mess. You don't treat a hearse like this. It ain't a good look. This hearse ain't rock'n'roll – it's straight graveyard material! But I'm about to bring this baby back from the dead.

" I'm in Cornwall, sitting in a hearse with an umbrella up! This ain't hip-hop...
**westwood**

# Please MTV, Pimp My Ride

Pimpee... *Jay Rotheram*

West Country rocker Jay wanted something a bit different for his ride. He ended up with a hearse, bought on eBay for £500. How come? "I used to watch things like the Addams Family and the Munsters and they'd have hearses with big engines hanging out the front," he says. "The Ghostbusters had one and I thought if I could get the equivalent of something like that, that would be awesome."

Jay and his band, Sin City, use the hearse – which saw 22 years' active service before becoming a rockmobile – to get to gigs, putting their gear in the back. "Rock music to me is everything," he says. His mission is to bring rock'n'roll to the South West, but that's not easy: the band live miles away from each other and there's not too many places to rehearse or gig in Cornwall. Sin City rely on Jay's ride.

But the hearse is held together with sticky tape. It smells, it rattles and it leaks: when Jay's mum is in the passenger seat, she puts her umbrella up. Having your mum sat in your tatty hearse with her umbrella up. What would Ozzy say about *that*? "Hearses are supposed to be big and black and shiny," says Jay. "But this thing sucks. I want to turn this hunk of junk into the hottest bandwagon in all of Cornwall!"

The guys at the garage haven't seen *all* the other bandwagons in Cornwall, but they think they can help...

## pimp dossier ...

>> **Name:** Jay Rotheram
>> **Ride:** 1983 Ford Granada Mark II Cardinal
>> **Lives:** Port Isaac, Cornwall
>> **Daytime:** entertainer (he says)
>> **Hero:** Slash from Guns N' Roses
>> **Loves:** cars, computers, travel. And rock. And roll.
>> **Is:** hard-working, entertaining, ambitious, outgoing
>> **Wants:** a car to help put Cornish rock on the map
>> **Also wants:** vintage hearse vibe of the Ghostbusters' Cadillac

# Pimp Plan...

"The hearse is a big car – so it's definitely pimpable. This one's done its job over the last couple of decades but the way it's looking at the moment, Slash wouldn't be seen dead in it. By the time we've finished with it, we're going to make it the ultimate rock machine. We know that Jay and Sin City struggle to find venues to play in Cornwall – so our aim is to turn the hearse into a venue in itself." **jamie**

"We know how much Jay loves the Ghostbusters Cadillac, so we're going to help him live the dream – we're going to give him his own set of Cadillac-style tail fins. Plus, for some extra bling, I'm going to chrome up the rest of the metalwork." **martin**

"This baby's going to be running on some flat-faced 18-inch rims that I'm going to wrap in some lovely low-profile rubber. Normally, the wheels I've chosen only come in black but we're going to custom-paint them white." **junior**

"I'm going to create a whole backstage lounge area for the band, with luxury cinema-style seats in the back and a DVD projector in the roof, so Jay and the guys can watch their favourite rock movies on the biggest screen you've ever seen in the back of a car." **bluey**

"If Jay wants to be a rock star, he's going to need to travel like one. I'm thinking snakeskin fabric on the seats and a wall, or rather, a ceiling of fame, with a massive collage of photos of rock legends looking down on him..." **pinky**

"I'm going to do the brightest, whitest re-spray you've ever seen – and then, to make it even hotter, it's going to be topped off with some scorching flames rising up from the grill." **ronnie**

# Pimping It

This was the first big car we got to work with on Pimp. We thought, "Right, we've got all this space, what can we do with it?" Instead of the normal four seats and a big boot at the back, we decided to put in a two-seater cinema. It was pretty mad. We've never done a Hearse before: getting parts was pretty difficult. We got some from a friend of Jamie's who uses hearses to go banger-racing!

## Exterior

- Chrome front and rear Nova 1967 bumpers
- Custom-made back box and exhaust TP32 with teeth for added nastiness!!!
- Rear lights painted white to blend with the bodywork
- Caddy-style fin lights with custom-made surrounds
- Chrome-embezzled quad front lights custom-made

" I added some tasty chrome up front, using a bumper I found on a '67 Chevy Nova – a custom classic. We got four new headlights with chrome bezels, then we custom-built a surround panel for each pair of lights out of metal and fibreglass. Finally, using the same method, we'll make some cool tail-fins, with torpedo lights. " **martin**

# Interior

"
We ripped out the mouldy roof that was making the hearse stink and replaced it with a rock Hall of Fame: there's pictures of rock legends. Ozzy's up there, Kiss, even Westwood. Is he rock? Is he a legend? Whatever. The whole ceiling is lit up by rock stars – and by the 44 red neon strip lights we put all over the interior. " **pinky**

● Purple polka, wine- and black-coloured leather from Andrew Muirhead & Son throughout

● Rear seats trimmed in plum snakeskin vinyl

● Front door panels re-fabricated/leather trimmed with angular speaker builds housing 2-way component speakers from JL Audio

● Front seats re-trimmed in black leather

● Cinema area with 2 rear seats facing a Sony VPL-ES2 data projector screen with DVD player

## Paint

- Re-sprayed in Brilliant White from House of Kolor
- Masked flames with red, orange and yellow fade-blended by Airstream
- New vinyl white roof
- Blacked-out windows

> To create some space, we had to grind out the old framework in the back of the hearse – and then we rebuilt it, making and installing new floors, walls and ceiling. This created a massive area to put in all the gadgets we had planned. The lounge has its own cinema with a DVD projector and electronic curtains – there's a subwoofer behind each seat and even more speakers, for total surround sound. And in the boot: an almighty PA system, with the most powerful PA speakers in the world with over 1000 Watts each. **bluey**

## Ice

- Blaupunkt Bremen MP74 Head units × 2 (front and centre)
- Blaupunkt DVD-ME2 player
- E25 amplifier mounted in the boot
- Also in the boot 2 × Resolution 1 speakers from Funktion One
- 2 × 12in JL Audio Subwoofers J12 W4 mounted behind the cinema seats
- JL500/1 mono amp and JL300/4 amp from JL audio
- 2-way component system enclosed in the front door cards CR635CSI

## Wheels

We custom-painted the 18-inch rims white to go with the rest of the paint job. junior

# Ford Granada Hearse Pimped

> Jay's hearse looked like it was ready for the big car park in the sky. But the guys at the garage have created an incredible bandwagon. It's a miracle! **westwood**

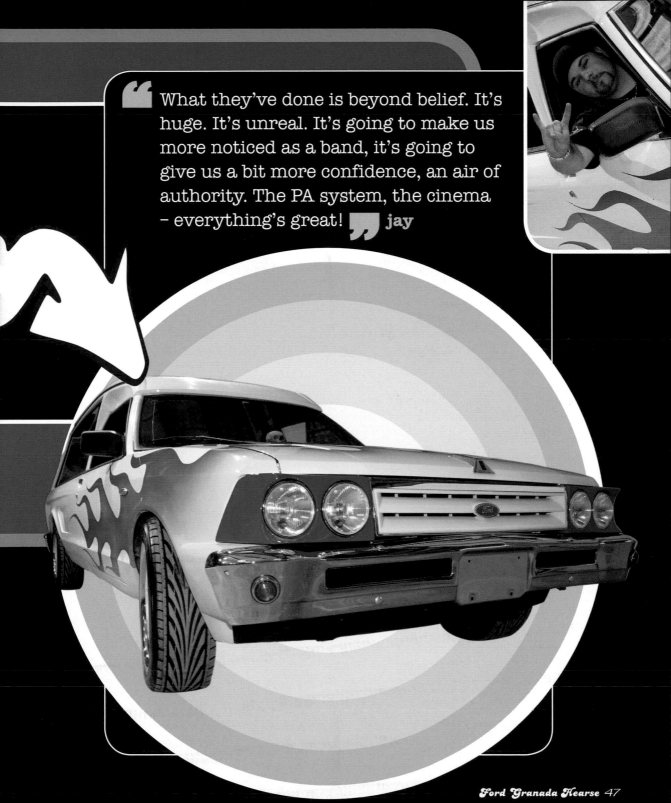

> "What they've done is beyond belief. It's huge. It's unreal. It's going to make us more noticed as a band, it's going to give us a bit more confidence, an air of authority. The PA system, the cinema – everything's great!" **jay**

# Bluey

## "Audio & Multimedia"

**You're the Pimp sounds man – so what's on YOUR system?**
It depends entirely on my mood. Anything from Metallica to Ella Fitzgerald. So it's quite a broad spectrum.

**What's your current ride?**
VW Corrado. It's not pimped.

**Have you ever pimped your own car?**
To a degree – but never gone over the top.

**Have you done embarrassing things, pimping-wise?**
Yeah, me and the Boss had to put girl's make-up on in the back of Lana's VW Polo... Jamie looked great in lipstick, ha ha!

**Favourite system put in a car in the Pimp series?**
The one that went into the Capri – it was just extremely loud. It shook the car.

**What's your favourite pimped car from the series?**
Lana's Polo. Aeroplane seats! It was one of those cars that didn't have a lot of gadgets and gizmos but still looked great.

**Where would we find you at 10pm on a Friday night?**
Ideally, I'd be on the beer, catching up with mates, having a laugh, that kind of thing. But if we're filming Pimp I'd still be working at the garage at that time.

**What's your favourite TV show?**
At the moment, I'm quite into American Chopper.

**How long have you been in the business?**
I've been getting paid for being a mechanic for about six years. But I've been doing it as a hobby ever since I've been driving. I'm 33 now.

Why are you called Bluey?
It's a nickname that stems from a
nickname that stems from another
nickname that stems from mine and
Jamie's childhood.

You've been pals with Jamie for years?
I'm Jamie's cousin.

Is anyone else in the garage related
to each other?
Not that I'm aware of!

What's your real name?
Stuart.

How many tattoos have you got?
Five. The latest one's on my right arm. It's
still peeling: I only got it done last week.
It's a Japanese coi carp: they're supposed
to bring you good fortune. They symbolise
strength and perseverance. Which is what
I've needed to do Pimp.

What are the others?
My first tattoo I had was an old girlfriend.
The next one was boredom.

It symbolised boredom?
No – I was bored! Then I've got the Carisma
garage logo on my back...

Fiat
Panda

# Please MTV, Pimp My Ride

**Pimpee...** *Armick Abolian*

Most nights, Armick Abolian and his pals are out skating and the ride that makes it all possible is Armick's 1987 Fiat Panda. Armick's been skating for 12 years, ever since he saw Michael J Fox in Back to the Future (apparently). He and the boys skate on London's South Bank most nights, but they've also been to Milton Keynes, Birmingham and Manchester to show off their tricks – all thanks to the Panda. It's not the obvious choice for a skater's car – but Armick loves Pandas: this isn't even the first one he's owned. "I just like the overall shape to them," says Armick. "They've got a funny character about them."

Some of the features on the current model aren't all that funny, though. But what do you expect when you buy a car for £50? The window on the driver's side keeps sliding down when he's driving; the doors are creaky; bits are falling off it; it's seriously uncomfortable.

Armick's Panda has always been tatty and uncool – but now things have come to a head. For three years, the boys have been planning a road trip round Europe. Everything's in place apart from the car.

"In this state, it'll never make it," says Armick. "It's basically a sardine tin with wheels on," says his mate Will.

What can Jamie and the boys do about *this*?

## pimp dossier ...

» **Name:** Armick Abolian
» **Lives:** Palmers Green, north London
» **Ride:** 1987 Fiat Panda 750cc
» **Daytime:** graphic design student, part-time lifeguard at swimming pool
» **Loves:** skating, Iron Maiden
» **Wants:** ride pimped so he can take the boys on a once-in-a-lifetime skating tour of Europe

## Westwood's verdict

Armick's board game is tight – but his car game is weak. Don't get me wrong: the Panda's cool for skateboarding wth his boys – but he's got no love from the ladeez. This car is crazy uncomfortable. It's got the worst interior I've ever seen in a car. The front seat crushed my hips; the back seat is a hammock...

" This is one Panda that's nearly extinct! This Panda is endangered! "
**westwood**

# Pimp Plan...

"At the moment, Armick's Panda isn't saying 'skater' to me one little bit. But I know we can give this thing some serious road presence with the custom-built body kit that I've got lined up. I don't think I've ever seen a Panda with street cred – but prepare to be surprised. **jamie**

"These guys are never going to get lost on their way round Europe. We're going for state-of-the-art GPS – plus a voice-activated translator. And just in case anyone's getting bored on the road trip, we're putting a games console and flip-down 10-inch screen in the back seat. **bluey**

It needs to look tough. We're going to go for some Urban Kandy green paintwork and then add some matching cool graphics to the sides and back of the car. Armick will love it! **ronnie**

Space and comfort are really important on any road trip. To make extra space, we're going for three seats instead of four: two seats in the front, one reclining seat in the back. **pinky**

We're going to take the limited edition body kit that I designed for the Renault 5 GT Turbo and rework it for the Panda. Every part will have to be modified by hand to make it fit. We're going to hook up the Panda with a trailer and a fold-out skate ramp so Armick can skate WHEREVER he is in Europe. **jamie**

The Panda's going to look tough – and the wheels can't let it down. The old wheels looked weak – but we're going to put on some wheels that are brand new on the market: 17-inch-ers – which is massive for a Panda – with a low-profile rubber. These wheels are not available in the UK yet, but we're having them made especially in the US. **junior**

# Pimping It

*This really was an awful car, with zero street cred – but the modified body kit came out really well, and the idea of having one seat in the back surrounded by speakers was pretty cool, too. We designed everything in it to look like ramps – even the speakers were all slopey and rampy.*

## Exterior

- Exclusive GT5R Carisma Automotive kit custom-made to fit
- Smoke-tinted windows from Nationwide Tints
- Custom-made trailer with fold-out skate ramps and grind pole produced by Wesbroom Engineering Ltd.

"We hooked the Fiat up with a trailer and two fold-out ramps. We went to a company that makes trailers and asked them to build something a bit different: first up, they built a seriously strong steel structure, then using plywood, they made two fold-out ramps and a grind rail. **bluey**

# Interior

"We got rid of the weird homemade scaffold-poles-and-canvas arrangement that Armick had for the back seats – and replaced it with three top-of-the-range, full carbon luxury sports seats. We used extra hard-wearing carbon fibre to reinforce the leather trim: I guarantee it will be able to take anything the guys throw at it when they're going round Europe. Finally, we made two compartments in the roof, fitted with neon lights – a perfect, custom-made storage space for the skateboards." **pinky**

- Nutmeg-coloured leather from Andrew Muirhead & Son throughout
- Wear patches trimmed in Culverhouse & Sons black carbon fibre-effect leather
- 3 new Cobra Misanos (2 in the front and a single seat in the rear)
- GPS system NVE-N099P from Alpine with TME-M770 screen, housed in the passenger's sun visor
- Alpine 9847 head unit
- Fabricated centre console with Ectaco TL-4 voice-activated language translator
- Switching panel to operate new components
- Flip-down 10.4in Audiobahn AVM104IRV screen for the reclining single seat in the back
- Fabricated roof cases, holding two Enjoi skateboards, either side of the rear seat lit by green neons

# Paint

- Re-sprayed in metallic Lime Green Kandy from House of Kolor
- Camouflage-style graphics by Image Worx laid over the back third

"We put some muscle into the Panda's sound system, with a remote control CD head unit up front, with TEN speakers powered by three amps fitted in a specially-designed half-pipe in the boot. The rad new system included speakers being built into the roof line... **bluey**

"We created a camouflage-style design, with vinyl layers stuck on to recreate the camouflage effect after the initial respraying was complete – a job that took 12 hours and 47 minutes worth of work. To be precise. **pinky**

# Ice

- Alpine 9847 head unit
- 6-disc CD changer CHA-S634 from Alpine
- GPS system NVE-N099P from Alpine with screen TME-M770
- 6.5 2 way Fusion component speakers × 3 in the roof
- 2 × 10in Fusion subwoofers FEW-10
- FE-402 Fusion amps × 3 with amp wiring kit K-AK4
- 10.4in flip-down Audiobahn AVM104IRV screen

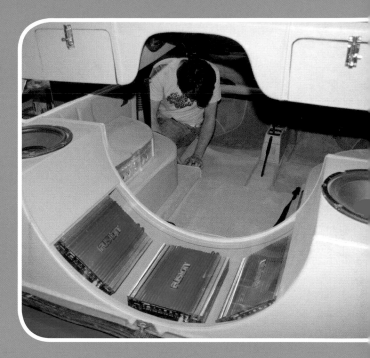

# Wheels

- 7.5 × 17in Bushidos from Wolfrace with Toyo Proxos 215/40/17 tyres all round

> **"** The road trip is definitely on. We've got the perfect car; the sound system is amazing. **"**
> **armick**

# Fiat Panda Pimped

"When I took Armick's car to the garage it was straight embarrassing. His Panda had no game. He was getting dissed. But the boys have blessed him with a strong look – he's going to be real big out there." **westwood**

# Pinky

## 'Design'

**What are you driving?**
My car is one of the new Beetles. I've also got a pink Vespa.

**Why Pinky?**
My real name is Karen but I'm called Pinky because I've been obsessed with pink since forever. I'm a girly girl. My house is all pink – well, all the accessories. They just had it in a homes magazine. They liked it because it was so pink.

**What are you listening to?**
I'm a grunger. I like my indie music. I like my festival music. I like the Kooks. I love them. I'm a band kind of girl. I'm going to see the Chili Peppers in a couple of weeks in Ipswich. I've seen them before and I love them.

**How long have you been pimping?**
I started working at the garage about six months before Pimp started. I'm a graphic designer by training. I work mainly in advertising and marketing when I'm not on Pimp. So instead of working on flat stuff, I'm working on 3D here, which is really nice. One of my other clients apart from MTV is Virgin Trains, I do a lot of work with them through my design company PinkCreative.

**Do you ever get recognised when you're out?**
I was in this little pub, dancing around, when these three blokes came up to me and just started chanting "Pinky, Pinky". I was quite scared. People come up to you and ask if you work on Pimp and when you

say 'Yes' they just walk off! That's their curiosity satisfied. As though they'd been arguing among themselves: "Bet it is/bet it ain't." But I normally get chanted at in the local areas: everyone in Colchester knows about Pimp my Ride, so it's only to be expected. I just try not to go to Colchester.

Who is Colchester's local celebrity?
Darren Day, maybe. Blur. Damon Albarn. We don't really have local celebrities.

What can you cook?
I eat steamed vegetables every day. I can cook anything. I love cooking nice food: I'm good at Christmas dinner.

What are you watching?
I love Big Brother... and I love Harry Potter.

What's the best piece of clothing you've ever had?
My favourite is probably the pink fluffy slippers my dad bought me for Christmas. They come up to my knees. I work at home so I always have my slippers on. What do I think about men who wear slippers? It's wrong. Men in suits are good.

Who would play you in the film of your life?
Drew Barrymore. She's just as squeaky and crazy as me.

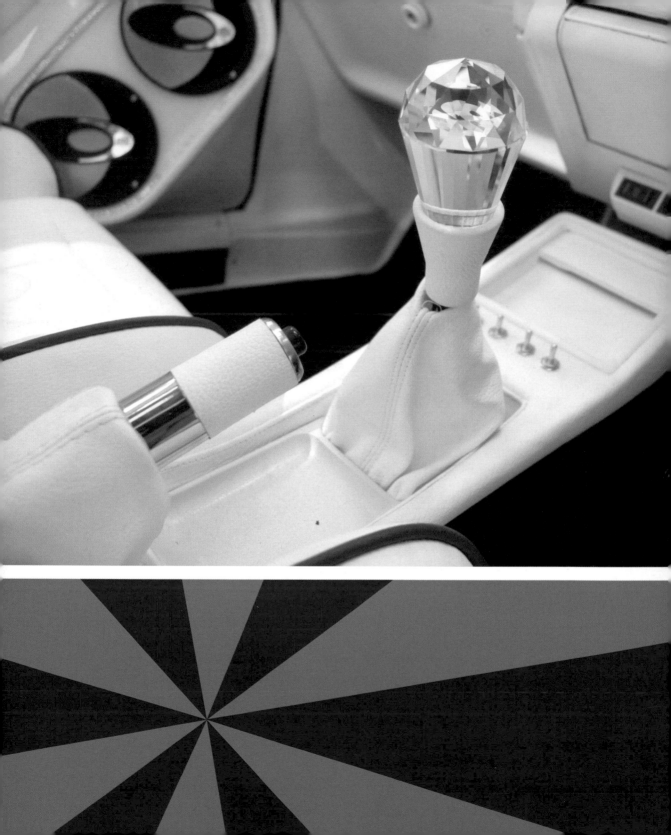

# Ford
# Capri

# Please MTV, Pimp My Ride

## Pimpee... Sean Egan

Sean Egan saved his Ford Capri from the scrapyard. But, though he loves the idea of his classic '80s boy racer ride, the reality is a little shabbier. By day, he's studying law; by night, he's shooting hoop. And the Capri's letting him down in both parts of his life. "When I go to play and pull up in the Capri, people look at me like I'm an idiot. They laugh at me, straight up! And if I turned up at court in this old banger, my client would definitely start sweating."

It all started so well: "The Capri is a classic British muscle car. I love Capris; I love the shape of them," says Sean. "So when I heard there was one going for sale at the local scrapyard, I thought: 'I'm having it.'"

But this Capri has taken a lot of hits: you can still see the jaw-marks on the top where the scrapyard lifted it down off the racks for him. He had an accident the week after he got it – the front end was hit, then the back end, then the front end again.

Sean's tried fixing up his rusty ride with tape, but that's not even a short-term fix. The front window's broken, the driver's seat is ripped up and the bodywork is a mess – especially the repair job Sean's done on the back end. Sean calls it three-tone: there's some rust there, some scraped paint and some body filler. It looks like raspberry ripple ice-cream. It's not a good look. What can the boys do?

## pimp dossier ...

- **Name:** Sean Egan
- **Ride:** 1986 Ford Capri
- **Lives:** Hampshire
- **Daytime:** A-level student
- **Loves:** basketball, playing guitar
- **Favourite year:** 1986
- **Is:** genuine, sweet, an honest guy, say friends
- **Wants:** a car that can be smart enough for his two very different lifestyles

## Westwood's verdict

Back in the day, the Capri was the hottest joint on the street. But don't get it twisted – that was 30 years ago! Now even the best lawyer would have a hard case defending it. This is a classic car and this is breaking my heart. Even the rubber is rusting! And it's full of rubbish, too. We all know the Capri is an old-school classic. But this car needs to go back to the scrapyard not the garage. This is more of a Ford Crapi than a Ford Capri. It looks like it fell out of the Ugly Tree and hit every branch on the way down. It's a straight mess.

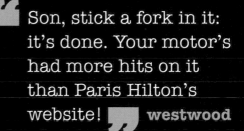

" Son, stick a fork in it: it's done. Your motor's had more hits on it than Paris Hilton's website! " **westwood**

# Pimp Plan...

> It's obviously seen better days, but the overall classic shape and feel is what I'm mainly interested in. By the time we finish, the Capri is going to be more showroom than scrapyard. Think class, think smooth, think bling. The UK may not have produced many legendary basketballers, but when it comes to muscle cars, we've always been serious players. Sean's Ford Capri may be a cult classic – but that doesn't mean we can't improve on it. **jamie**

> We're going to lose this old bonnet and put on a new one with a phat power-bulge made out of the old bonnet. No other Capri in the world will have a bonnet like this! **martin**

> Right now the Capri's paint is flaky. We're going to re-spray it Cobalt Blue Kandy to light up the streets – a total of 18 coats! It's going to look amazing – but we have to be extra careful painting with Cobalt Blue Kandy, because every little mark on it shows. **ronnie**

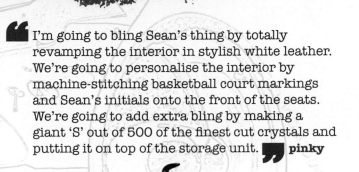

> I'm going to bling Sean's thing by totally revamping the interior in stylish white leather. We're going to personalise the interior by machine-stitching basketball court markings and Sean's initials onto the front of the seats. We're going to add extra bling by making a giant 'S' out of 500 of the finest cut crystals and putting it on top of the storage unit. **pinky**

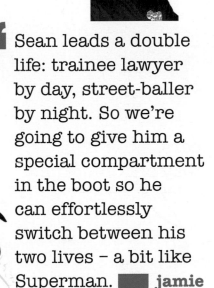

> Sean leads a double life: trainee lawyer by day, street-baller by night. So we're going to give him a special compartment in the boot so he can effortlessly switch between his two lives – a bit like Superman. **jamie**

> We're fitting a pop-up electronic scoreboard in the boot. In fact, we're going to ram the boot with kit: we'll put in a games console loaded with top basketball titles. Plus we'll have 2400 watts of power from two subwoofers. **bluey**

> We're going to give Sean some big and bling rims: rather than just studying the law, he's gonna be the law! We're giving him 17-inch chrome beasts – chromes do not get any hotter! Instead of going from A to B, Sean's now going via Bling Central. **junior**

# Pimping It

One of our favourites: a classic car painted in a cobalt blue – and the white interior just sets it off nicely. Plus it has a big sound system. Each car on Pimp takes three to four weeks to do, from start to finish (on the TV show, this is compressed into about four minutes!). There's generally 10 of us in total who work on every car, even though only six or seven of us appear on TV.

## Exterior

- Front and rear Mk5 Escort Cosworth bumpers customised to fit from Pro Sport
- New standard lights with extra fog lights on the front bumper
- RS2000 Ford Escort side skirts from Pro Sport
- Custom-extended bonnet power bulge
- Webasto deluxe 300 soft touch electric sunroof with rain sensor closing
- 3in outward roll stainless trim custom-made exhaust from Exhausts UK

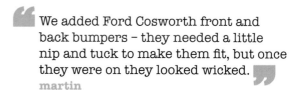

We added Ford Cosworth front and back bumpers – they needed a little nip and tuck to make them fit, but once they were on they looked wicked.
martin

# Interior

> We lost the back seats and made the Capri a two-seater instead. The extra space was used for the rotating storage area, with a cylindrical wooden unit fixed on a rotating bearing. The basketball kit can sit in one half – and Sean's legal garb in the other half. **pinky**

- Bright white leather from Yarwood throughout, including headlining with blue piping on the seats
- 'S' logo embroidered onto top of seats with machine basketball court design on the base and top of the seats
- Black carpet trimmed with white leather edging throughout
- Front door panels re-fabricated/leather trimmed with angular speaker builds housing 2 way co-axial speakers from MTX Audio
- OQO Model 01 ultra personal computer housed in front centre console, with flip-over mouse mat from armrest for Logitech V500 wireless mouse
- Custom-made 100% crystal 'pimp stick' gear knob with engraved 'S' logo inside from Swarovski
- 2 front dials and speaker builds in the door cards surrounded by Swarovski crystals
- Custom spinning storage area in the centre of the back with personalised 'S' logo on top made from 500 Swarovski crystals lit by blue Fuel neons. Storage area contains shirts, ties and cufflinks from Thomas Pink on one side, and basketball clothing from AND1 UK on the other.

## Paint

- Re-sprayed in a base silver and a Cobalt Blue Kandy from House of Kolor

"The gear knob was custom-made by the finest crystal engravers – with an 'S' cut into it, too. We also gave Sean smaller, individual crystals around his dials and around the speakers in the front doors. And the blinging car has a blinging head unit, too: perfect for the man about town, it not only pumps out sounds through the massive sound system we installed but also works as Sean's mobile phone all the time he's in the car. We got Sean the smallest, hi-spec laptop in the world: he used to have a mouse in the car, and now he's got another one. No more need for scruffy folders or notebooks – this laptop is one of the first of its kind to hit the UK. It's a serious piece of kit." **bluey**

# Ice

- FHL-17 Sony 17in LCD screen
- Exclusive Pioneer DEH-P70BT Bluetooth head unit, working in conjunction with Sony Ericsson K700i mobile phone from Orange
- Sledge Hammer MTX Audio dual Thunder 5500 12in subwoofers
- Thunder 3404 – 4 channel amp and Thunder 3401 – class D mono-black amp from MTX audio supplied by BBG distribution
- StreetWires cabling, fusing and accessories throughout

# Wheels

- 7.5 × 17in chrome Hybrid from Wolfrace with Toyo Proxos 205/40/17 tyres all round

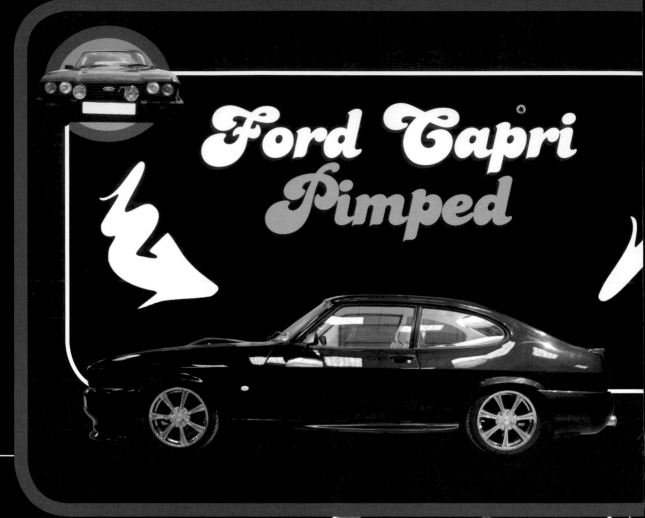

# Ford Capri
## Pimped

The guys have gone all out and slam-dunked this baby. Now the only thing this car is guilty of is looking fabulous.     **westwood**

> "The way my Capri looked before, I just wanted to hide, I was embarrassed. But now I love it so much – it's amazing to have something so special. It's great to have something this beautiful. I feel like a king." **sean**

## "Accessories"

**What's your speciality?**
I'm a bit of an all-rounder; I can rub a panel down; I can do a bit of welding: I'll help with anything. But I've been fitting car stereos for years and love doing complicated installs - when Bluey's not already finished the job! I completely overhauled my own stereo and now it rumbles.

**What do you do apart from pimping?**
DJing is the love of my life. I've been DJing for 15 years. I've played every genre of music – house, garage, drum n' bass, hip-hop – to perfect all styles. I do a lot of club work. I do the Hippodrome in Colchester on Tuesdays – they're always a laugh – and TALK in Southend. I'm pretty well known in Essex. I play a lot in London too, and am best known for appearing at the major modified car shows. I mixed a cover CD for Max Power magazine and the Ministry of Sound disc "Maximum Bass" which was specially for the cruisers and went to No. 3 on the album charts. That pretty much made my year!

**What are you driving?**
I've had some phat bikes and then I got hit by a car. So, as much as I love bikes, I'm trying to lay off them because they're dangerous. I've got a black BMW 330 E46 and it's fully pimped out with 20-inch rims, a carbon air-filter, carbon bonnet, performance exhaust, leather interior,

3 TVs, a monster sound-system, sat nav, DVD, MP3, CD, Clifford alarm and the icing on the cake – my 'Richie Don' DJ logo embroidered in the headrest. I love it.

**What was the first record you bought?**
When I was 12, me and my mate went fishing and found a box of records in a skip: most of them were wrecked. The only one that wasn't was Julio Iglesias. A few days before I'd seen the DMC Championships on TV: I was amazed at what the DJs on were doing. So I rode home on my BMX with my Julio Iglesias record and tried to scratch

it on my dad's turntable. And it sounded crap! I couldn't understand why it didn't sound like the guys I'd seen on the telly! The joyful journey started there!

**How many pairs of shoes have you got?**
I don't wear shoes – I live in trainers. I've got around 20 pairs, all of them mint except my work ones. My philosophy is – the more trainers you have, the less wear n' tear they get!

**How many records have you got?**
At present around 5500-6000 and growing, Not bad for a DJ.

**What can Westwood learn from you as a DJ?**
Garage! Westwood never played it. I rip my parties down with it! Tim is a pioneer and a legend in the hip-hop scene and many younger readers won't know that. We've done gigs together in the past where all the guys from the garage have come along. One time at Ignite in Basildon when I was nearing the end of my five-year residency, I DJ'd immediately after Westwood and together we smashed the building to bits – it was a fine moment in my career!

**What is the one thing you would wish for?**
There's not enough hours in the day. If it were a 36-hour day, that'd be wicked.

# Black
# Cab

# Please MTV, Pimp My Ride

## Pimpee... Bez

When Happy Mondays/Black Grape dancer/mascot Bez won Celebrity Big Brother in 2005, the first thing he said, after 17 days in captivity, was that he wanted his ride pimped. He'd gone on the show to help pay his tax bill. When he won, picking up £10k extra in prize money, he decided to spend his winnings on his ride.

Bez had saved his Black Cab from the scrapheap and, putting it nicely, it was ripe for pimping. In fact, before MTV even got to him he'd already started spending his cash with a little self-pimping. "I put a seven-litre Chevy engine in there and a race gearbox – it sounds like a race car and it goes like a race car," he says. But while the engine may be as good as it gets, everything else is pretty shabby. Paint flaking off on the outside. Holes in the bodywork and the inside. The sunroof doesn't open anymore. Not just that: the yellow 'For Hire' light's gone as well. So Bez can't pick up any fares. Imagine that!

"It's got the most ugly looking wheels you've ever seen in your life," says Bez. "And it's got a plastic wing-mirror with black installation tape holding it in place. The wipers don't work... But apart from all that, it's lovely and I like it!"

Bez can't wait to see what the boys come up with: "I've always got bored of me cars," he says. "But this one's special and I'd love to give it a new lease of life..."

## pimp dossier ...

» **Name:** Bez
» **Ride:** 1988 Black Cab
» **Daytime:** being Bez
» **Claim to fame:** tallest Celebrity Big Brother winner (previous winners: Jack Dee, Mark Owen)
» **Loves:** maracas, freaky dancin'
» **Trivia:** Bez's dad was a police detective inspector!
» **Sounds:** currently fronting Domino Bones

## Westwood's verdict ...

This beat-up and destroyed cab was on the way to the scrapyard: then Bez gets it and spends 10 grand on it – and it doesn't look any different. Right now, Bez is destroying himself. He's spent all his money putting a monster engine and exhaust system into a pile of junk. It's a 1988 cab sitting on a cruise missile. It feels crazy powerful: it's got some real muscle but it looks like a piece of scrap. It's more shabby than cabby. It's ugly, it's bust – and it's disgusting... Come on, understand: this is *Bez*, the ultimate party animal!

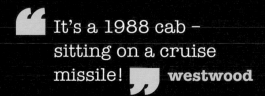

“ It's a 1988 cab – sitting on a cruise missile! ” **westwood**

# Pimp Plan...

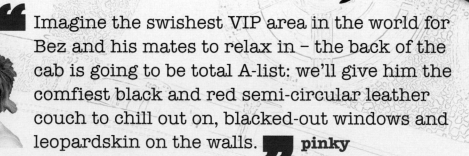

"It's got a nice big space inside – there's big arches, suitable for big rims, so there's plenty of scope for us here. By the time we've finished with it, it's going to be the most expensive ride in the world: we're going to build him the ultimate party pad – on four wheels. **jamie**

"For all the entertaining Bez is going to be doing in here, he's going to need a ton of gear. I'm putting a giant plasma screen inside for playing games and watching DVDs. Add to that some smaller screens up in the ceiling. This car is going to be 100 per cent psychedelic. **bluey**

"Imagine the swishest VIP area in the world for Bez and his mates to relax in – the back of the cab is going to be total A-list: we'll give him the comfiest black and red semi-circular leather couch to chill out on, blacked-out windows and leopardskin on the walls. **pinky**

"I'm going to hook up some top DJ gear up front, so that when Bez and the boys come out of a club they can just keep on keeping on." **jamie**

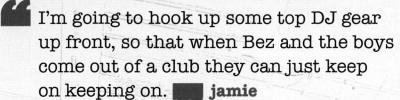

"Paint-wise, I'm thinking deep, deep purple – plus we're going to brand the back with Bez's own freaky dancer graphic... **ronnie**

"It's going to need a red-hot grill: it's going to be big, blinging and blinding, pure Rolls-Royce style, with a mini-cam tucked inside relaying pictures of the outside world to the big screen in the back." **richie**

# Pimping It

Bez was the only pimpee who'd had anything serious done to his car before we got hold of it. In the real world, most people who customise their cars get the engine done first. On *Pimp My Ride*, we concentrate on everything but the engine. We do little things: we always put on a high-performance exhaust and we change the spark plugs, too. Trust us, though: Bez's engine didn't need any tweaking.

## Exterior

- New headlights with chrome surround
- Wing-mounted chrome round mirrors
- Custom handmade Rolls-Royce-style grill with mini camera mounted on to the top (for viewing on the screen in the back of the taxi)
- Converted taxi-hire light to flash 'PIMP' on red background

 We installed a tiny camera inside the custom-made Rolls-Royce-style grill linking to the plasma screen in the back, so Bez and his mates can sit in the back and watch the world go by, without having to look out the window. And, in contrast to the deep purple paintwork, we lined the roof with dark-red snakeskin vinyl and then finished the whole thing off with a graphic of Bez's freaky dancer logo on the boot – with some extra snakeskin trim on the bumpers too! **jamie**

# Interior

"Inside, we fabricated a wooden frame for the base of the curved couch. Then we trimmed the seats in black and red leather. The leather has added lycra which means it is stretched to fit the seats perfectly. The hand-stitched design we gave Bez would normally only be seen in the world's most expensive prestige cars. We built in a motorised seat that slides out from under the dashboard, for the in-car DJ booth." **pinky**

- Smoke machine in boot which pumps into the VIP section

- New black carpet laid throughout with red leather trim around the edge

- Mini cocktail area with ice bucket and champagne flutes

- Xbox clear housed under the plasma

- 4 Laser crabs and 2 strobes hidden in the back wall for a nightclub effect

- 1 head unit and 2 DVD players from Blaupunkt

- Red and green neons from Fuel lighting different areas around screen and speakers

## 𝒫aint

- Re-sprayed in Purple Pearl from House of Kolor
- New claret snakeskin-textured vinyl roof with custom matching front and rear snakeskin bumpers
- Blacked-out windows to side and rear
- Boot covered in Happy Mondays' 'Freaky Dancin' logo customised graphic

- Blaupunkt TSA 1300 Amps × 4 and TSA 460 × 4
- 2 × DVD-ME2 Blaupunkt DVD players
- Woodstock DAB54 Blaupunkt digital radio/CD/MP3 player
- TSx693 3 way triaxial system 210w Blaupunkt speakers × 13 with back lighting kits
- 14 × IVMS-6502 6.5in colour TFT-LCD Blaupunkt monitors
- 3 × Blaupunkt TSw300 transparent high-power speaker 600w single voice coil 12in subwoofers
- Blaupunkt TSw250 transparent high-power speaker 540w single voice coil 10in subwoofers × 3
- Sony plasma 42in screen KE-P42M1
- Numark DXM01USB-240V 24 bit mixer

# Ice

" We put a 42-inch plasma screen in the back, hooked up to a games console and two DVD players. Plus we hooked up 14 mini-screens in the ceiling. In the back, we installed a wall of sound – three 12-inch subwoofers, three ten-inch subs, seven speakers in the couch, six in the door, all powered by eight amplifiers: it's like a nightclub on wheels! **bluey**

" Up front, we fitted the standard 16-inch-rim wheels but at the back, we've got 18-inchers. This gives the cab a nose-down stance, almost like a hot-rod. **junior**

# Wheels

- Front: 16in chrome hubcaps with Toyo proxos 195/50/16
- Back: 7.5 × 18in Chrome Matrix from Wolfrace with Toyo proxos 225/35/18

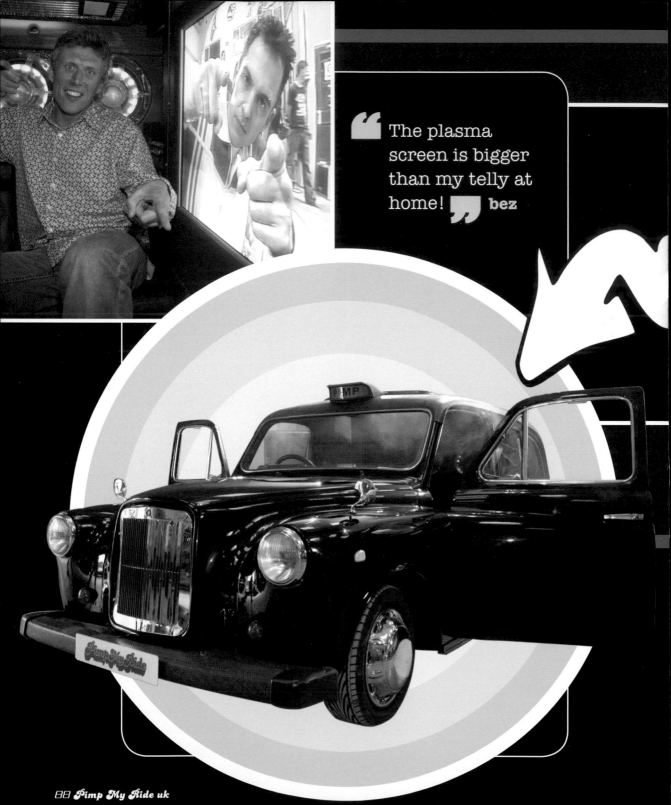

The plasma screen is bigger than my telly at home! **bez**

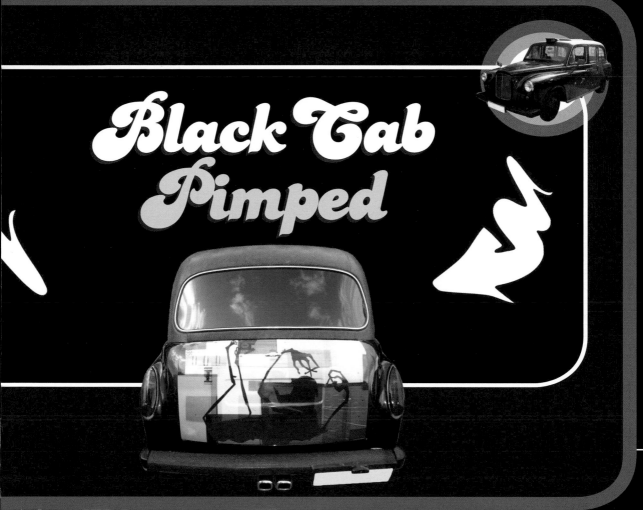

# Black Cab Pimped

It's very Bezzy. He's going to get shown crazy respect out there. It's like the ultimate mobile disco! **westwood**

# Westwood in the area

**What's your story with Pimp My Ride UK? How did you get involved?**
I'm a straight car person: my access point into the car game is from a hip-hop perspective. I'm a dude who loves big trucks – chromed up, rimmed up, painted up, tricked out with a massive sound system. I like all that creative non-factory modification.

Throwing on big rims is one thing: but with my trucks it's all that creative car customisation – putting on extenders so the wheels stick out more; changing the bonnets to something more mean-looking; adding an extra bumper with four sets of fog lights; taking off the side trim and the roof rack to give it a sleeker, faster look; losing all the black rubber by colour-co-ordinating everything. And mandatory 24-inch exclusive rims sitting on low pro-rubber.

I love Pimp My Ride, the US version as an inspirational car show. So when the Pimp My Ride franchise was developing I was with it from the jump. They asked me to come in for a screen test. I'd never auditioned or demoed for anything in my life. For the screen test, I walked around a car, talking about it. It was the producer's car: I was surprised at what a messed-up car he had! There was moss growing on it! They asked me to come in and make it happen.

**Are you a good driver?**
Yeah – very much so. The thing with me is that when I drive - I've got hot whips, man: I want to drive slowly so people can see them. I don't want to drive past at 100 mph so they say, 'What was that?'. I drive slow. Simple as that. I want people to really absorb the full flava of what I'm rocking, the power of my joint.

**How many cars you got?**
Five. Every fleet has to have a classic, that's what separates new money from the unobtainable – new money can buy a lot of things but you can't buy classics. I think I've got the hottest car in the UK – a '66 Chevy Impala, fully restored, in red Kandy, looking incredible.

**The UK show's funnier than the US one, isn't it?**
What you gotta understand is that the UK show has its own identity: the mechanics are very much what you experience in the car game over here. Ronnie is the type of guy who will spray your car, whether it's on TV or under a railway arch in South London. Jamie is the real deal when it comes to tricking out joints. So that's got a very UK perspective to it. And the pimpees are all very UK and the cars are the type you see on the UK road. And I'm UK, so it's only natural it would have its own identity.

Some of the guys in the garage fancy themselves on the turntables. Have you seen them in action?

Yeah: those cats love scratching. They'll just scratch like some people play video games – Junior, Richie, Jamie. Relentless scratching. They'll put a drum n' bass track on and scratch for two hours. It can be a mess.

# Nissan Sunny

## Westwood's verdict

Chris has got healing hands – but not when it comes to his car. It's a wreck. If you're into reliable cars, it's always worth checking out a Nissan. But a word of advice: if it looks anything like Chris's – don't do it to yourself. His is just straight busted and battered. Even Stevie Wonder can see what's wrong with this car! Congratulations for winning the Sunny, son. But you ain't won jack...

> **This car is just stupid. It's the worst car we've ever had!**
> **westwood**

# Please MTV, Pimp My Ride

**Pimpee... Chris Herodotou**

Reggae-lover Chris won his 1988 Nissan Sunny in a game of poker. "The kitty was the car – it was the grand prize and I won it," he says. Not a bad night's work, you'd think. But how would he sum up his grand prize? "It sounds bad, it smells bad. And it looks quite bad as well," he says. Ah.

Chris qualified as a massage therapist a year ago and worries that the Sunny doesn't create the right impression when he pulls up to clients' houses: it doesn't look professional. The clock doesn't work, which means Chris is always late for appointments. But that's the least of his worries. He may keep his massage table in the back but the Sunny itself looks stressful. In fact, the Sunny's in such a state, it looks like it's been abandoned. People graffiti it and – when the clingfilm fails and that window slips down – the local youth dump rubbish in it. Cheers.

Chris wants to leave his clients chilled – but he's a sunshine boy: he loves the beach and his dream is to go to the carnival in Brazil. Failing that, he wants to boom out some chilled reggae sounds from his ride. Fat chance of that right now.

"Without my Sunny, I can't do the job I love," says Chris. "But while I'm out there curing people's aches and pains, my car is just causing stress." Can the boys at the garage help him take better care of business?

## pimp dossier ...

- » **Name:** Chris Herodotou
- » **Lives:** Southgate
- » **Daytime:** massage therapist
- » **Loves:** reggae, sunshine
- » **Hates:** "commercial music that's all about status and attitude"
- » **Car's name:** Edu, after the Brazilian football star
- » **Ambition:** to be in the British Olympic team for London 2012, as a masseur
- » **Looking for:** a Caribbean sunshine feel to his Sunny

# Pimp Plan....

"The future is so bright, Chris is going to have to have his shades on by the time we've finished with this." **jamie**

"We're going to add an executive body kit from a Volvo – but we're going to custom modify it for the Sunny." **jamie**

"We need it to be as bright on the outside as Pinky's planning to make it on the inside: so we'll turn it Brazilian green all over, with a little yellow fade down the side panels." **ronnie**

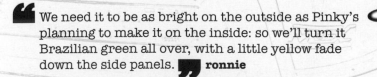

" You can't have a beach party without some serious sounds. So I'm going to be giving Chris a truly bass-thumping system. Then I'm going to give him his own personal supply of sunshine – by putting an SAD light in the glovebox. **bluey**

" Chris loves the Caribbean; he loves Brazil. So we're going to give him his very own patch of beach – real sand, in fact – right here in the front of his car, with a false floor in the front and the back. We'll light it using red neons to give it a nice warm glow. **pinky**

" I'm going to give it some high-powered 18-inch silver rims, with specially designed centre caps – with lucky Jacks into the middle to represent the poker game that won Chris the car. **junior**

" First up, we have to get to grips with the doors. I don't like the look of those holes for a start. Then I'm going to build up his body strength with a custom-modified body kit. **martin**

# Pimping It

One of the things that took the longest to get right was the boot. We wanted to get an urban feel to it and we didn't have any materials to cover the install – then we thought of calling our mate Pro 9 who's a graffiti artist and a DJ. We got him to do a few graffiti sketches, with a Hawaiian, tropical, Jamaican kind of feel. Once the install was complete, we sprayed it up, job done.

## Exterior

● Bodykit by Erebuni. Style number 313 DTM Volvo 850
● Ecosse twin fog lights
● Twin 3.5in Pipe back box from Exhausts UK

"There were so many messed-up panels on the car, we got a second-hand Nissan in mint condition and used the doors and perfect body panels off that. The front bumper of the Volvo body kit was way too wide, so we cut it down to size – then blended it in with the top half of the Nissan's own bumper. Then we made some fresh apertures for two very stylish new fog lights." **martin**

# Interior

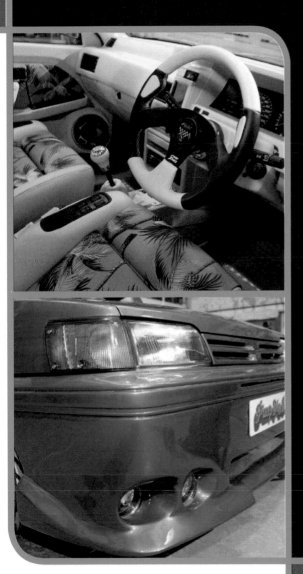

"To continue the tropical feel, we gave Chris yellow-tinted windows and trimmed the seats in aztec yellow leather, with contrasting palm-tree fabric on the back panels for the ultimate beach party on wheels. The front seats are orthopaedically designed so that Chris doesn't end up on the massage table himself; the centre arm-rest on the back seat has two bongo drums built in. **pinky**

- New Recaro Orthopead seats in front
- Door panels and centre panels of seats covered in Hawaiian 'Waikiki' print fabric from Barkcloth Hawaii
- Andrew Muirhead & Son 'Aztec Yellow' leather on seat surrounds
- New sports steering wheel XR 330 LY, trimmed in leather, from Auto Inpart
- New electric Webasto sunroof
- Sand-filled clear plastic footwells from Project Plastics lit with red LED bars from Varad
- New chrome gear knob and chrome pedal set 860PGX from Auto Inpart
- SAD therapy light-box LTSAD001 fitted into glove box, supplied by Allergy Matters
- Vestax Handi Trax portable turntable (in boot)
- 3 × 15in MTX subwoofers supplied by BBG Distribution (in boot)
- Boot interior spray-painted in beach graffiti by Pro 7 Graff (in boot)

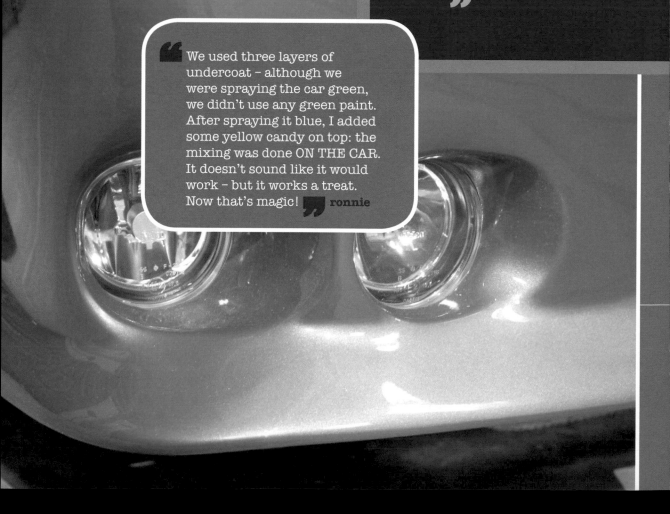

## Paint

- Main body re-sprayed in Lime Gold from House of Kolor.
- Executive stripe and fade in matt yellow by Bee Bee Refinishing Supplies
- Yellow window tint by Tintman

A sound system for a reggae lover needs to be loud, proud and full of bass. So we put four amps and three 15-inch subwoofers into the back of the Sunny to give it that authentic Dancehall sound – plus a turntable for playing the old-school 7-inches on. All of it's hooked up to a head unit in the front of the car, playing CDs and MP3s. Plus we've installed six-and-a-half-inch-wide screen monitors into each head rest, hooked up to a games console, so you can watch DVDs or play poker. **richie**

We used three layers of undercoat – although we were spraying the car green, we didn't use any green paint. After spraying it blue, I added some yellow candy on top: the mixing was done ON THE CAR. It doesn't sound like it would work – but it works a treat. Now that's magic! **ronnie**

## Ice

- 2 × 6.5in headrest screens. Sony XVM-F65WL
- XBox playing Bicycle Casino from Zoo Digital Publishing
- Wireless MEX-R5 CD head unit from Sony
- Full closure alarm from GAP Security a Clifford Arrow 5
- New massage table from Therapy 2000
- Palm Life Drive personal organiser supplied by Kaizo

## Wheels

- 7.5 × 18in Drift from Wolfrace with Toyo 205-40-17 tyres all round
- Custom designed 'Jack' vinyl centre cap made by Premier Signs

It's amazing. The car will definitely improve my business. Potential clients will think I'm a cleaner, better person because I'm not turning up in a rust bucket! I've never had anything like this in my life! **chris**

# Nissan Sunny
## Pimped

You've got the hottest Nissan Sunny in the world! Everyone will want Chris's hands on them now! **westwood**

# *Ronnie* "Paint"

How long does it take to re-spray a car?
The average time, if we're doing a Kandy, is about 16 or 17 coats. I've got it down to a fine art now: it only takes four or five hours to paint with the top coat. Not including the rubbing down and all the preparation with the primer. With all that, it takes a full day. We don't do anything too extreme with the paint on Pimp because of the time factor – we can't multi-colour a car or custom-paint it like we could in the real world. We can't do a 'flip' on Pimp – that's the prism effect you can get, so the colour of the car seems to change as you move around it, from green to red to yellow.

What have you learnt from Pimp My Ride?
After doing Pimp, I've got a bit more respect for actors.

You're a football fan, aren't you?
I'm East London born and bred: I support my local team and always have done. I used to have a West Ham season ticket when I lived in London. Yeah, I would say that West Ham supporters are the best supporters. The most loyal anyway. We've played some crap over the years, but we still averaged 20,000 fans – and 30,000 in the Premiership.

Sven-Goran Eriksson. Discuss.
I wasn't a Sven fan. The best thing about him being England manager was his retirement. In a perfect world, the England manager would be Terry Venables. Without a doubt.

How long have you been working on cars?
All my life since I was 17. Off and on. You

walk away from it for a while. It always drags you back, once it's in your blood.

**What's your ideal Friday night?**
Years ago, it was getting in at four in the morning, having a couple of hours' sleep and getting up and playing football. Now, it's going out and having a laugh with my mates. Maybe having a kebab on the way home. And not playing football the next day.

**Who does what on Pimp?**
We all do a bit of everything, but 90 per cent of my work on Pimp is the paint.

**Do you have a secret skill?**
I'm good at drinking beer.

**What are you watching?**
My favourite films are the Godfather trilogy. If you want to sit down and watch a serious film. That and Lord of the Rings. I like films that you watch and you know at the end that there'll be a sequel.

**What do you think of Big Brother?**
You've got to be brain dead to watch Big Brother. Surely?

**Who would play you in the film of your life?**
In the film of my life, I'd be played by Bob Hoskins.

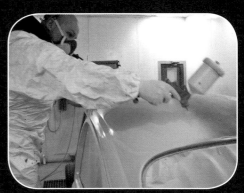

BMW
316

# Please MTV, Pimp My Ride

## Pimpee... Adam Bridges

Hip-hop fan and accounting student Adam Bridges says he's been unlucky with cars. He only passed his driving test four years ago but he's already been through nine cars. Adam's tenth is a BMW 316 series. "Just another in the long list of terrible cars I've had," he says, glumly.

It's got dents all over the place, bits held on with tape, and Adam can't even *get into* the thing with any dignity. "I have to climb in from the passenger side because the driver's door is broken," he says.

The BMW has no radio: Adam gets his music via his portable MP3 player and some headphones. The sounds are strictly hip-hop. The system... isn't. And the state of the car is only going to get worse. "I'd like to say I was a good driver but I'm not really sure if I can," he says. "I misjudged a wall going into a car park and knocked the badge off..."

In his spare time, Adam is a bit of a fitness fanatic: he goes weight-training and has a special interest in the Korean martial art Tae Kwon Do. He ferries two pals to classes, with all their kit spilling over from the boot into the back seat. Being a student, that back seat is also full of old takeaways and general rubbish. "I actually like the car - it's my friends that don't," says Adam. "They all laugh at it."

What can the boys at the garage come up with?

## pimp dossier ...

» **Pimpee:** Adam Bridges
» **Ride:** 1989 BMW 316
» **Lives:** Kingston-upon-Thames
» **Daytime:** accountancy student
» **Loves:** being a fitness fanatic
» **Spare time:** Tae Kwon Do
» **Ambition:** become a black belt within 12 months
» **Sounds:** hip-hop
» **What's he like:** friendly, helpful. The Beemer is already his Tae Kwon Do club's main transport

## Westwood's verdict

BMW? Bob Marley and the Wailers? It's a bit more...
Shaggy. Inside, it's a mess: it looks like student
accommodation in here! It's got dents. It's got tape
all over the place. Adam is a cool guy but his BMW 316
is a piece of junk. He's into hip-hop and Tai Kwon Do
– in other words, he likes music and kicking people.
But his ride is making him look real weak out there.
Adam treats his BMW like student accommodation:
unwashed clothes everywhere, bits of old food. It's
nasty; it's disgusting; it's not hip-hop. The guys at the
garage need to bless him with something special.

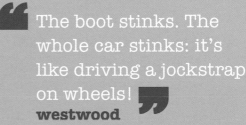

" The boot stinks. The
whole car stinks: it's
like driving a jockstrap
on wheels! "
**westwood**

# Pimp Plan...

"When I saw we had a BMW to work with, I was a very happy man. It's only a 316 but that shape and style is a very classic gangsta-style and all the guys are really looking forward to working on it. We've decided to go for something that's classy and a little bit bling – a US low-rider style... **jamie**"

"I'm going super hi-tech on this one. Adam's getting the very latest car computer in his dashboard: it'll play MP3s, CDs, DVDs, plus it's got WiFi internet access, satellite navigation, the works. Knight Rider's kit, with 2Pac's style. It's all linked up to a touch-screen display. Plus I'm going to build a Tae Kwon Do mobile training centre in his boot! **bluey**"

"We're going to straighten out all the panels and fit a phat body kit. **jamie**"

Adam's BMW is seriously lacking flava – but I reckon some chocolate leather and sprinkling of walnut will change all that. It'll look good enough to eat. We'll put walnut on the dash, on the doors and on the centre console: we'll go to town, and make the interior look more like an executive suite than student accommodation. **pinky**

Seats-wise, I'm going to give Adam an old-school look. First I'm going to re-foam the seat backs of the old chairs – then I'm going to re-trim it with chocolate-brown leather. **jamie**

We're to have sky-blue pearl for the body and a contrasting white vinyl roof. **ronnie**

I'm going to give Adam some super slick 'suicide' doors – doors that hinge the 'wrong' way, a bit like the new Rolls-Royce Phantom. These can be pretty tricky to install: effectively we have to make the rear doors open the wrong way round. We have to cut the hinges off the front of the door – and add new hinges on the BACK of the door. **martin**

# Pimping It

*Our favourite gadget on this one was the Karputer head unit, which looks like any other CD head unit but holds a full Windows package in it. That, together with the mobile Tae Kwon Do unit we set up, with its embedded webcam-style camera and 15-inch screen, should be reason enough to not go misjudging walls.*

## Exterior

- Front bumper and side skirts supplied by Raid UK
- Rear bumper supplied by Rieger
- Custom-made exhaust supplied by Exhausts UK
- M3 wing-mirrors and baseplates supplied by Raid UK
- Angel Eye headlight conversion supplied by Quality BMW Online
- Chrome wheel arch trim supplied by Eurocar parts
- Aerial supplied by GK Motor Factors
- Suicide door kit supplied by Showtime Automotive

"The suicide doors took a lot of work. We used one singular hinge: normally there'd be two, but we were restricted by the shape of the back doors. We had to realign, cut and weld for what seemed like forever until finally we achieved the perfect fit." martin

# Interior

"To make the mobile Tae Kwon Do training centre, we first made a reinforced steel cage in the boot, then put two punch-pads on it, hooked up to two hi-tension springs. There's a webcam-style camera in there and a 15-inch screen, so the guys can watch themsleves training and pick up on any mistakes they're making. We also put in three kit lockers, so there's no excuse for smelly kit." **bluey**

- Walnut interior film on dash supplied by FDT Technics / Foliotek
- Walnut steering wheel and boss supplied by Raid UK
- Gearknob and leather handbrake lever and gator supplied by Raid UK
- Brown leather for dash and cream leather supplied by Yarwoods
- Brown thread supplied by Culverhouse & Sons
- Beige Lamonta fabric for seats supplied by Boynetts
- Parchment Bison Vinyl for the roof supplied by Boynetts
- White Dial Kit (400sg) supplied by Lockwoods international
- Seat buttons supplied by Franklins
- Brown carpet supplied by Munchner Autostaff
- Blue 12in LED bars (HLW15BL) for boot supplied by Drivecast
- 2 × wine coolers supplied by drinkstuff.com

## Paint

- Blueberry Pearl paint (DP42 over BC26), base coat and lacquer supplied by House of Kolor

> " We had a lot of problems with this: we were spraying Blueberry Pearl over a white base coat but it kept going opaque. Eventually, I mixed my own baby-blue base coat and put the Blueberry Pearl over the top of that. Mint. " **ronnie**

- 1 × Ice Pac 2 Computer supplied by Karputer
- 2 × 7in motorised screens supplied by Spot Technologies
- 15in (MR1542) LCD screen supplied by Blaupunkt
- 2 × 6.5in Audiobahn Speakers (ACIS62) and 2 × Audiobahn 10in (AW101T) supplied by Tech Distribution
- 1 × Audiobahn 2 Channel Amp (A1502DP) and 1 × Audiobahn (A1004DP) 4 Channel Amp supplied by Tech Distribution
- 1 × Audiobahn Sub (AW100T) supplied by Tech Distribution
- Colour Bullet camera supplied by Automotive Styling
- Nintendo DS games console with Mariocart supplied by Nintendo

## Ice

"The Karputer head unit looks like a normal CD head but it also had a full Windows package on it, full hard-drive navigation as well as playing CDs and MP3s. It can do anything – we're going to be seeing a lot more of that kind of kit in cars in the future." **jamie**

"I gave Adam 18-inch, 120-spoke chrome rims so he can really rock with the big guys! These will knock out all-comers. They are classic hip-hop, and flown in direct from the States." **junior**

## Wheels

- 17in Radial Lace Wheels, supplied by Dayton Wire Wheels
- Toyo tyres 205-40-17

> Driving it is like a dream, really. It's not a situation where I have to keep my head down anymore, in case people see me. I'm going to spend more time in the car than in my flat! I feel really lucky. **adam**

# BMW 316 Pimped

> This car's got some serious muscle now. Adam's looking hot in the street in it. — **westwood**

# Junior

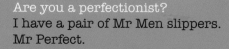 'Wheels & Tyres'

**How long have you been working on cars?**
I've been in the business four years now.
I'm 19. I did work experience at the
garage and stayed. And stayed.
And stayed.

**Why Junior?**
Everyone calls me Junior but my real
name's Stuart. Everyone used to call
the other Stuart here – Bluey – "Roo", and
I was called "Roo 2". It's got changed
to Junior.

**Are you a perfectionist?**
I have a pair of Mr Men slippers.
Mr Perfect.

**What can you cook?**
I can cook anything: chili con carne, roast
dinners, anything.

**What do you say to people who claim that
you suggest the same thing for every car?**
Sod off. What is there to say? You're always
going to want the biggest wheels possible
and you're always going to want chrome.
It's standard.

**What's your favourite piece of clothing?**
I had some Gap jeans that I modified into
Gucci-style jeans with rips and bleached
bits, did all the reverse stitching on the
sewing machine in the garage. Jamie
started off customising his clothes and
everyone followed.

**What are you driving?**
I've got a beautiful old Beetle that I'm doing
up; my dad bought that for me. Whatever
the others tell you, I've only crashed one
car. The other car I had, I blew up – then
someone stole it and crashed it.

**What is your ideal Saturday night?**
My ideal Saturday night? Usually, we
start sitting round mine with a few mates

and have a few bevvies. Then go down the local pub, have a few games of pool, get a few more drinks in, have a go on the fruit machines. Then into town, have a few more drinks, see what women are about. Then walk home.

Can you do any impressions?
I can impersonate Donald Duck. Martin can do Scooby Doo.

Which team do you support?
I'm not into football, really. But I do watch England.

What is your middle name?
I won't tell you my middle name.

What's your favourite film?
Scarface.

What are you listening to?
My favourite music is hip-hop – and hardcore drum n' bass. We've always got the decks going downstairs while we're working. Richie is a professional DJ – me and Jamie are just mucking about.

Who would play you in the film of your life?
In the film of my life, I'd be played by Johnny Depp.

# VW Camper Van

## Westwood's verdict

On the real? I'd rather go to jail for a fortnight than go on holiday in a Camper Van. This is not a happy Camper. It's like a giant tin can. It's a real messed-up situation. I'm not feeling good about it at all. No disrespect to Zoe's Grandad or her Dad – but this is junk. Zoe's Camper Van has been in the family for three generations. But if it's going to survive another it's time for some drastic action. We've got to turn the 'Beastie' into a beauty.

" Camping in Lowestoft? That's where I'm from, man: the mean streets of Lowestoft - East Coast, Baby " **westwood**

# Please MTV, Pimp My Ride

**Pimpee...** Zoe Waller

Hippy chick Zoe and her Camper Van go way back. All the way back, in fact. Zoe's Grandad bought it in the late '60s and he passed it over to her Dad – and family legend has it that Zoe was actually conceived in the Van. "I feel a bit embarrassed about that," she says.

But when Zoe's mum got MS, her dad no longer had the time to look after the Camper Van. He passed it on to Zoe: she says she's a real '70s girl, so she loves having the original hippymobile as a ride. She's even given it a name – 'the Beastie' – and she and her boyfriend used it to go camping every year in Lowestoft – until it just got too dilapidated.

The Camper looks grey: rusty, old and flaky. The windscreen leaks; the curtains are discoloured and there's mould round the windows because of the water coming in. "I don't wash the van because when I do the paint comes off," says Zoe.

Zoe's a PhD student but her real love is painting and drawing. She's even tried a bit of brushwork on the Camper: the front of the Van is pristine. She says that job took her four months. What size brush was she using?

Zoe's whole life is tied up in this Camper Van. It's been in the family three generations but, right now, a fourth would be pushing it. "This Van means the world to me," she says. "I've got to get it back on the open road."

## pimp dossier ...

- » **Name:** Zoe Waller
- » **Lives:** Ipswich
- » **Ride:** 1967 VW Camper Van
- » **Daytime:** studying chemical biology for PhD
- » **Likes:** 1970s, camping, art
- » **Extras:** very crafty. Makes cutomised cards, blankets – and trousers for her boyfriend
- » **Inspiration:** Gwen Stefani
- » **Sounds:** punk, ska
- » **Wants:** ride to survive into fourth generation of her family

# Pimp Plan...

" The Camper Van is a classic. We can really do some serious pimping on this. It's got problems but they can be rectified. It looks dull, like a breezeblock on wheels. Theme-wise, we love the fact that Zoe was conceived in the Camper, so we're going to create her very own modern love-shack: it'll be like a honeymoon suite – including a sofa that turns into a bed at the flick of a switch... " **jamie**

" I'm going to give Zoe her very own hip hotel on wheels. In the back we're going to have a pair of giant red lips that turn into a sofabed – and along the side an ultra-slinky white lacquer cabinet that wouldn't look out of place in the slickest design magazine. Plus we'll add in some lighting that Zoe can control to suit her every mood. " **pinky**

" We're going to give Zoe plenty of screens, to keep her and her boyfriend entertained on their trips. We'll put one in each of the slide-back doors, so Zoe can sit outside and watch films on a summer's night – plus one in the ceiling for those nights in when you just want to cuddle up and watch a movie. " **bluey**

> I'm thinking chrome. And lots of it. Plus we're going to sort out Zoe's leaking roof. We're going to let the sunshine in through four new panoramic sun roofs. **martin**

> I'm not going too hi-tech on this one: I'm thinking pure comfort zone. I'm going to fit Zoe up with a remote control teasmaid in the back – so she can brew up from her sexy sofa bed. Plus I'm going to install a weather-forecaster in the front, above the dashboard. **richie**

> If you're going to go camping in this country, you need to take the sunshine with you. I'm thinking of sparkling Gold Kandy all the way down the sides – and on the roof – and on the front, contrasting cream **ronnie**

# Pimping It

Sourcing parts for any of the Pimp cars can be a problem – they're all old. But with a 1967 Camper it was never going to be easy. Where do you find a roof for one? We had Richie and Junior on the phone to the US and Europe – no dice. We ended up getting one from Lakeside, about 30 miles away.

## Exterior

- Chrome wing-mirrors supplied by Custom and Commercial
- Chrome side-trim kit supplied by Creative Engineering
- Chrome VW badges for front and rear supplied by Coolair
- Family tree on rear window vinyl produced by Premier Signs
- Roof replaced, new roof supplied by Big Boys Toys
- Heart-shaped exhaust supplied by Exhausts UK

"The old roof was a rotting mess: there was nothing we could do with it, so we tracked down a replacement – and then cut it to accommodate four panoramic, state-of-the-art sunroofs. On the body, everything that could be chrome IS chrome. We gave the Camper the classic US-style chrome bumpers, got a polished chrome side step – and a brand new chrome badge. **martin**

# Interior

"Oddly enough, you can't get lip-shaped sofas for Camper Vans, so we worked our magic on a standard seat. We cut the plywood seat backs into the lip shape – and built in some linear actuators to make it open and shut at the flick of a switch, turing it from a sofa to a bed. We also gave the Camper its own sophisticated mood-lighting system, building in eight nine-inch colour-changing light-bars with over 1000 different colour settings. Plus we installed over 225 fibre-optic strands above her bed. Finally, we gave Zoe a golden dashboard and trimmed the seats and door panels with the finest cream Italian leather – and laid a deep-pile purple carpet throughout." **jamie**

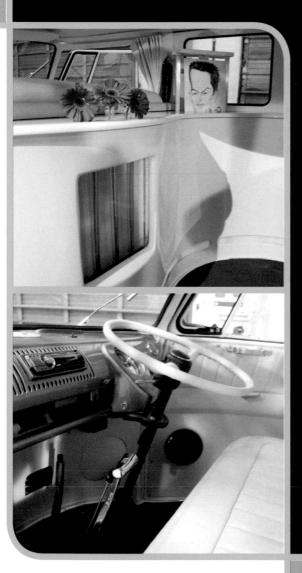

- Easel supplied by Testrite US
- Rear window tinted black, tint performed by Tintman
- Under-unit changeable lighting – Perspex supplied by Project Plastics, lights and controller supplied by Drivecast
- Motorised lips rock-and-roll bed trimmed in red alcantara, and fabricated from an original bed supplied by Custom Made Furniture. Linear actuators supplied by Select Products
- Teasmaid from Russell Hobbs
- Panels between windows trimmed in cream leather, with cream curtains
- 2 × Webasto Hollandia 500 panoramic sunroofs supplied by Webasto
- Fibre optic back wall, optics supplied by Optic Lighting

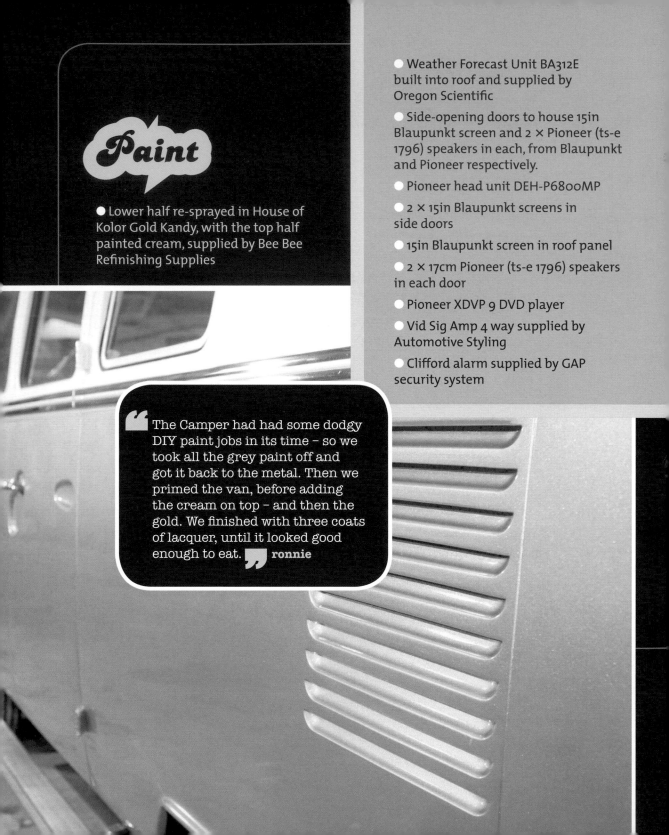

## Paint

- Lower half re-sprayed in House of Kolor Gold Kandy, with the top half painted cream, supplied by Bee Bee Refinishing Supplies

- Weather Forecast Unit BA312E built into roof and supplied by Oregon Scientific

- Side-opening doors to house 15in Blaupunkt screen and 2 × Pioneer (ts-e 1796) speakers in each, from Blaupunkt and Pioneer respectively.

- Pioneer head unit DEH-P6800MP

- 2 × 15in Blaupunkt screens in side doors

- 15in Blaupunkt screen in roof panel

- 2 × 17cm Pioneer (ts-e 1796) speakers in each door

- Pioneer XDVP 9 DVD player

- Vid Sig Amp 4 way supplied by Automotive Styling

- Clifford alarm supplied by GAP security system

> The Camper had had some dodgy DIY paint jobs in its time – so we took all the grey paint off and got it back to the metal. Then we primed the van, before adding the cream on top – and then the gold. We finished with three coats of lacquer, until it looked good enough to eat. **ronnie**

## Ice

"Everything – lights, music, films, teasmaid – can be controlled from a bedside control panel, with the 15-inch screen in the ceiling above the bed. Plus, when you're on your way back to the Camper, you can get the mood just right via your mobile phone, which can turn on the low-level mood lighting, the twinkling back-wall lights – or move the bed into position. To top it all off, we installed a water feature inside of the lacquer cabinet: very Austin Powers." **bluey**

"Finding new wheels was not an easy business. On a '67 Camper the wheel studs are twice as far apart as on a standard car wheel – but I found some 15-inch fire spokes that should keep the Camper going for another 30 years." **junior**

## Wheels

- 15in EMPI Wheel – MP5 spoke polished supplied by Big Boys Toys
- Tyres size 185/60/15 supplied by Toyo

It looks amazing and I feel amazing driving it. It's hard to remember what it looked like before – it's just so different. You can see it coming a mile off. It means everything to our family, it really does ... **zoe**

# VW Camper Van Pimped

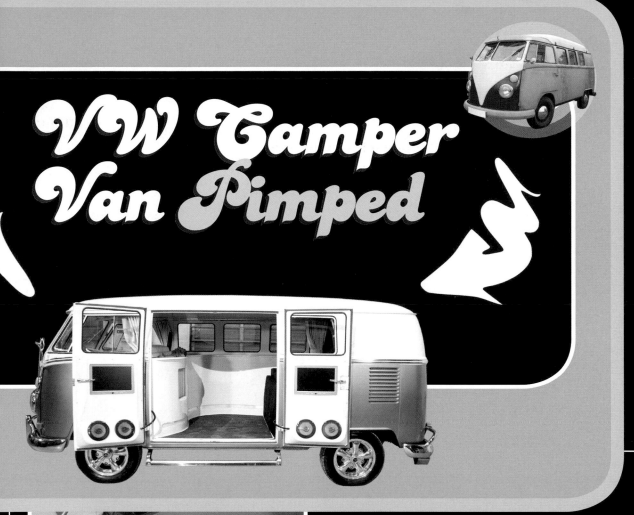

> " The Camper Van was straight trailer trash – but the guys have transformed it into a penthouse on wheels. **westwood**

 **'The Boss'**

**You've been pimping for a while, haven't you?**
I've been doing this for 13 years now. I was working at Rolls-Royce and while I was there, I started building modified custom cars as a hobby – and I had so much success, in terms of getting editorial coverage in magazines: I was getting publicity money couldn't buy. When I was 19 I had a car at the Motor Show that I'd built myself. I had cars on magazine covers while I was still working at Rolls-Royce. So I took the big step of starting to work for myself. And in the nine years before Pimp My Ride, we went from strength to strength and became Europe's most reputable car modifier. And then Pimp My Ride was like the icing on the cake.

**How did working at Rolls-Royce help you in learning to pimp?**
Everyone at Rolls-Royce had their own specific job to do – if you worked in the paint shop, you were there for 40 years doing that and you were the best at your trade. There was no sideways movement. To me, that was quite limiting. So, while I was doing my own stuff at home, I'd go round to all the guys there and ask them for advice: if I wanted to trim a door panel, I'd go and ask them the best way to do it. So I got the best knowledge from the best people. But I'm predominantly self-taught in everything I've done. And then I've passed my knowledge onto my guys.

**What marked you out from other guys customising cars?**
I've got a different perspective on building cars to other people. Most guys that build a car will look through a magazine, choose some wheels, side skirts and window tints all from different places and then put them together: they don't look at the thing as a whole, about how all the parts and colours complement each other.

**Are you really into art and design in all areas? What about your house?**
Oh, yeah: I've got several projects on the go in my house. I have a massive eye for design and craftsmanship generally, not

just in cars. Almost everything I do is about self-contentment, really. I'm not trying to prove anything. I admire anyone who dares to be different. Hats off to them. Even if what they do is atrocious and everyone hates it, at least they've had a go.

**Has anyone ever asked for anything ridiculous, pimping-wise?**
Apart from MTV?! No – MTV's fun. Pimp My Ride is like being given a blank canvas, with just an outline on it. But the work we do on Pimp My Ride isn't typical of the work we do generally. In the real world, people won't spend £25,000 on a £100 car!

**What kind of money DO people spend on customising their cars in the real world?**
We've had a guy spend £50,000 on one car – and £100,000 in total. He had a complete one-off body kit for a TVR Tuscan, plus some audio and upholstery work and a complete respray. It was about four months' worth of labour for three or four guys. A TVR Tuscan is a very individual car to be driving round in anyway. But his philosophy was the same as mine: you can have all the money in the world and you can buy whatever car you want, but then you could pull up at the traffic lights and have exactly the same car pull up next to you. So his way of expressing the fact that he had a lot of money was to say, 'Yes I have this individual and unique car that's now even more individual and unique'.

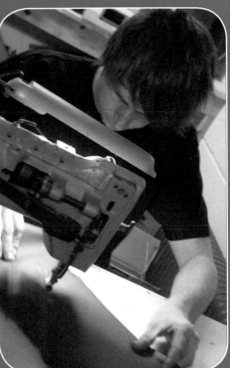

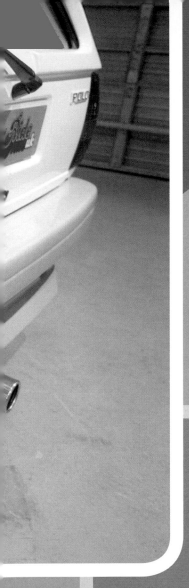

VW Polo

# Please MTV, Pimp My Ride

## Pimpee... *Lana Inglis*

Party girl Lana is an air hostess but her VW Polo is about as far from the jet set as you can get. And now she's had enough. Her ambition is to pilot her own private jet but at the moment she's just ferrying her friends to parties on Friday and Saturday nights in a 15-year-old Polo.

Lana says she always wanted to *fly* a plane rather than work as cabin crew on one. "I drive my friends round all the time – why not fly them around?" she asks, semi-plausibly. "The next step for me is to get my private pilot's licence. But it's a question of money. I've got to save up hard for that."

The Polo's party lifestyle means that it's full of leftovers: unfinished takeaways, old pizza boxes... shoes. "It's a bit of a bomb site at the moment," says Lana. It's worse than that. The body work is full of dents, the worst one being the result of a collision with a supermarket trolley in a high wind (Lana says it wasn't her fault). The sunroof is broken: passengers have to sit on bin liners because the seats get soaked with rain. The heater, meantime, is uncontrollable, with no setting between frozen and roasting.

How would Lana sum up her sense of style? "Glam luxury. And luxury glam," she reckons. "And that car is a part of my life that doesn't seem to fit me... To get the Polo pimped would be fantastic. It would be the most amazing thing that's ever happened to me in my whole life ever..."

## pimp dossier ...

» **Name:** Lana Inglis
» **Lives:** Edinburgh
» **Ride:** 1990 VW Polo
» **Daytime:** air hostess
» **Extras:** saving up money to train as a pilot
» **Family:** brother is UK karting champ. Lana drives all over the country to watch him race
» **Trivia:** Lana's Polo was originally owned by the Queen's cousin!

## Westwood's verdict

Lana loves the glamorous life but her Polo ain't built for that. It's not repping her image. It doesn't feel good, there's bits falling off it, I don't understand it: Lana is a glamorous chick, but there's nothing glamorous about this. It's about as glamorous as getting the bus. The whole thing is just plain nasty.

> There's glitter and hair-dye all over the seats. It's like a tart's handbag.
> **westwood**

# Pimp Plan...

"I'm going to install a screen in her sun visor to play back hidden camera footage of her mates' shenanigans on a Saturday night – and she's going to be able to record it with her own in-flight black box. We'll put a 'bullet' camera hidden in the roof and Lana will have her own screen built into the sun visor too – her friends will need to show a bit more respect for the Polo now. **jamie**

"We're going to change the shape of the Polo with a customised body kit. To make it more aerodynamic I'm fitting it with specially adapted spoilers. We'll also fit a new front grill and side skirts. **martin**

"We're going to give Lana Club Class and a Class Club all rolled into one for her and her crew to enjoy: we're going to replace her old seats with real Boeing 747 seats, re-trimmed in the style of a luxury Limo." **pinky**

"Every dolly needs her trolley – I'm going to custom-build Lana a mini-trolley for all her clubbing and make-up needs. Plus, I'm going to black out the back windows, to keep the party in full swing." **bluey**

"I'm going to widen her wheel arches and give her some jet engine-style wheels." **junior**

"Picture a very small private jet mating with a very small Limousine – we're going to make this Polo look like their baby! We're going all aerodynamic with this one: new streamlined bumpers front and back, smoothed-off door handles and, in the spoiler, its very own landing lights. It's going to be symmetry in motion." **richie**

# Pimping It

The hardest part of this one was putting the Boeing 747 seats in – it's not every day you put aircraft seats into a car. Obviously, an aircraft seat is usually mounted slightly higher off the floor in a plane; in a car it needs to be slightly lower. So Bluey and Matty reworked all the sub-frame mountings to go into the floor to make the 747 seats sit properly in the Polo.

## Exterior

- Bodykit: supplied by PSG Bodystyling
- Angel Eyes front lights supplied by GBK Performance
- Door handles removed and bodywork smoothed off to improve aerodynamics. Doors open on pop-locks supplied by Gap Security
- Side skirt neon 'landing lights'. VARAD SL 200 LED BARS supplied by Drivecast

"The main exterior work was in fitting the customised body kit which, with its spoilers and side skirts, changed the whole shape of the Polo. We also gave Lana extra 'landing lights' under the side skirts. I also filled and smoothed over the door handles to create the smooth look of a plane: the Polo now opens via some special 'pop-locks'. We also replaced Lana's tatty old exhaust with a chunky new centre-exit one. **martin**

# Interior

"The Boeing 747 seats we had flown in from the States didn't fit the Polo, so we had to cut them down to fit – and then re-trim them in colours to match the outside. We kept the picnic-tray in-flight tables in the back of the seats and added other airline-themed touches including 'No Smoking' and 'Fasten Seatbelts' signs... **pinky**

● Four genuine Boeing 747 seats, from Southern Aviation Services, San Antonio, Texas, USA

● Seats padded out for a luxurious ride and re-upholstered in a combination of raspberry- and wine-coloured leather from Andrew Muirhead & Son

● Chrome 'Universal Rally' pedal set, 'Winner' gearknob and new sports steering wheel X2 33 with Elegance Universal handbrake lever all from Auto Inpart, with tailor-made handbrake gator and steering wheel re-trimmed in grey and raspberry leather to match interior seats

● Ceiling re-trimmed in Lamonta Blush suede from Boynett

● Grey-coloured carpet for executive limo look

# Paint

Our plane-inspired paint job began with painting the whole car brilliant white, then spraying the bottom half in metallic silver. Finally we added two raspberry-coloured go-faster stripes – and a customised airline-style logo for Lana on the side. **ronnie**

- Limited edition 'Pimp My Ride' sick-bags supplied by Flightstore
- Tartan lambswool blankets in 'Lindsey' tartan from Scotweb
- New luggage set from Antler. Model 'Smart' in pink
- 4 × screens fitted to view DVDs and in-car CCTV footage
- DVD player SAV DVD built into glove box from Fusion
- Front-loading CD head unit SCD 255 S from Fusion
- 4 × 17cm 2-way co-axial marine speaker in white FSM 65 – FPS 652
- Internal Coga PA system and musical horn supplied by Demon Bikes

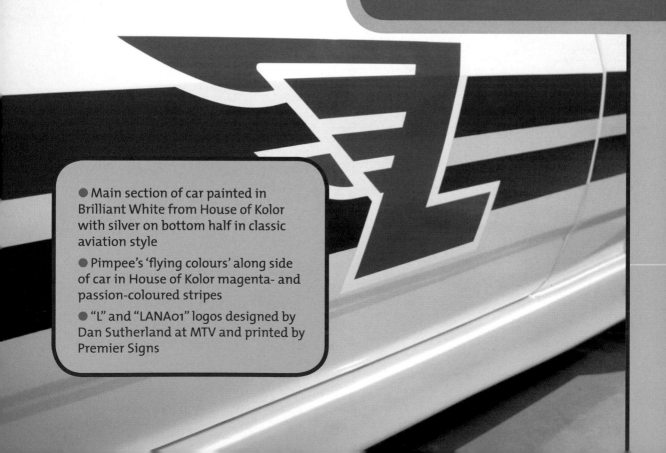

- Main section of car painted in Brilliant White from House of Kolor with silver on bottom half in classic aviation style
- Pimpee's 'flying colours' along side of car in House of Kolor magenta- and passion-coloured stripes
- "L" and "LANA01" logos designed by Dan Sutherland at MTV and printed by Premier Signs

## Ice

I built an in-flight trolley for her passengers, with snacks, drinks and a whole beauty section, too. The trolley wheels out from a hidden compartment between the two back seats. Overhead toggle switches in the 'cockpit' control everything in the car including a DVD player and a new stereo. We gave Lana her own airline-style internal PA system – and put a mirror ball in the roof. **bluey**

We fitted a new body kit to beef up the wheel arches; then we fitted chunky 17-inch chrome wheels. So the Polo is ready for lift-off. **junior**

## Wheels

- 7 × 17in Chrome Jet X from Rimstock with Toyo 205/40/17 all round
- Wheel arches widened with G60 arch kit to improve car profile

This car is so me. It's hot. It represents glamour, pure style. Wherever we go now, we'll go in absolute luxury. It feels like I'm in the cockpit of a proper plane and I love it! Absolutely love it... **lana**

# VW Polo Pimped

> The Polo's ready to take off. It was mad shabby, falling apart – but now it's ready to touch the sky! **westwood**

# Martin "Bodywork"

**What was the hardest thing you had to do on Pimp?**

I'd never done those suicide doors before. I had to work it out for myself. It took me two weeks. And then when I'd sorted that, we passed it over to Ronnie – and he had even more problems with it. That was the car with the mos... challenges on it, shall we say?

**Is your own car Pimped?**

I've done quite a lot to my own car, but haven't gone overboard. I've got an Alfa Romeo: a nice set of wheels, got rid of all the scratches it had on it when I bought it. I've got a spoiler on the boot, body kit on it, modified the grill and colour-coded a few of the interior bits, so they match the outside...

**What's your favourite car from the series?**

The Camper. It just looked so good: an older vehicle that's been brought up to date rather than being completely modernised or modified. The colours looked right, the

features in it were right, everything. It had lots of ideas and goodies in it, but they all fitted the vehicle.

Do you get pestered by fans?
I did get recognised at an airport once – by two kids. "That's that bloke off the telly." But that's been it.

Are most of your customers men?
I reckon about 40 per cent of our customers at the garage are women.

Is Pimp my Ride good for business?
Well, it's good for enquiries. You get a lot of people ringing up. But out of every 30 enquiries, you probably get one job. That's the scale of it. People get to know our company through Pimp my Ride.

How do you relax?
I enjoy watching action films and I listen to Radio 1.

What can you cook?
Curry. Chicken curry, beef curry, lamb curry. And egg and chips.

Who would play you in the film of your life?
In the film of my life, I'd be played by Nicholas Cage.

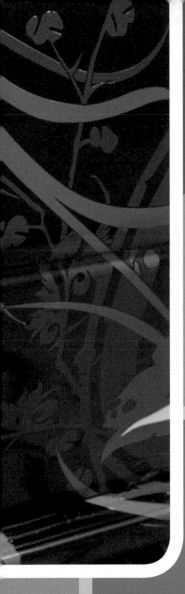

# Suzuki Swift

## Westwood's verdict

Jamie wants to make it big in Tinseltown but turning up
to auditions in the Swift ain't helping him get any parts.
This car is really stripped naked – where's all the kit?
Where's the trim? I thought he LOVED his car – he may as
well just cut the lid off, paint it yellow and call it a skip.

**" I see no evidence
of this being a good
car. ,, westwood**

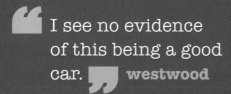

# Please MTV, Pimp My Ride

**Pimpee...** *Jamie Stallwood*

Struggling actor Jamie has had his Suzuki Swift for a year. Right now, he works as an usher in Brighton's Theatre Royal and he fears that if he keeps turning up to auditions in his Japanese rustbucket, he'll never get any closer to Tinseltown. "I wanted a car that was a bit fast and stylish," he says. "But this hasn't got any of that! I sort of fell in love with it when I first bought it. To see what it's turned into now is quite depressing."

The Swift's front window doesn't open properly; there's rusty holes in the side panels; the front passenger seat collapses when you sit in it. Jamie *did* get some side skirts for the Swift, but the welding is beyond him, so he's dumped them in the boot rather than putting them on the car.

Jamie has a big interest in Japanese culture. "I love the country, the culture, the calligraphy and I love the cars especially: the way they look; the way they sound; the Japanese are so far ahead in technology..." Being an actor, Jamie's other big love is movies, especially British gangster films. His favourite actor is Danny Dyer, star of Human Traffic.

His friend, Laura, likens the Swift to a bin on wheels. But Jamie has a big sense of style and the guys in the garage should be able to help him. "To drive round in something that I'm proud of owning would really be a confidence boost," he says. "I'm never going to get a starring role in this!"

## pimp dossier ...

» **Name:** Jamie Stallwood
» **Ride:** 1991 Suzuki Swift GTI
» **Lives:** Burgess Hill, Sussex
» **Daytime:** actor, barman/usher at Theatre Royal in Brighton
» **Loves:** Brit gangster films. His favourite actor is Human Traffic star Danny Dyer
» **Also loves:** Japan – the culture, the people and the technology
» **Inspiration:** Bruce Lee
» **Is:** funny, chatty, always helping out his friends

# Pimp Plan...

" I love working on Japanese cars; they're wicked for pimping. And my initial reaction upon seeing the Swift was that it was a wicked car – but in a bad way. Jamie had a Japanese car, all his influences are Japanese – so we decided to go for an awesome Japanese street-racer look... " **jamie**

" I'm going to sort Jamie out with a street-racer look that he'll definitely be proud of, by fitting a special new body kit. " **martin**

" Jamie's a massive film fan so what could be better than building him his own cinema in his car? On command, Jamie's bonnet will elevate and illuminate: and a projector will blast his favourite movies onto it, so all he has to do is park up and relax... " **bluey**

"I'm going to fit a state-of-the-art head unit that's come in from Japan – he sold his last head unit to keep his car on the road, and that's dedication that deserves rewarding." **jamie**

"The car's red right now – but it's not hot. So we're going to paint it black and then cover it in the coolest Japanese-inspired graphics that you've ever seen – plus I'm going to design Jamie his very own Hollywood-style wall of fame in his boot for a little silver screen inspiration." **pinky**

"Acting's a tough world, so Jamie needs all the help we can give him. I'm going to link him up with a digital camcorder built into his dash, linked to a seven-inch screen. so he can rehearse his lines and then watch himself back, wherever he is. **richie**

# Pimping It

One thing we learned from pimping the Suzuki was that a lot of graphics on the outside of the car is a simple but cost-effective way of opening people's eyes on the street. Don't always think about special effects paintwork – maybe consider using some wicked graphics. If you get the design right you can have a really eye-catching car.

## Exterior

- Jetspeed Bodykit supplied by Evofusion
- White LED lights (SL200) for projector screen provided by Drivecast
- Japanese-style exhaust supplied and hand-crafted by Exhausts UK
- Bonnet rising 8in linear actuator supplied by Select
- Under-bonnet projector display-panel provided by Carisma
- Japanese/Manga-style graphics created by Engine Design

> You can't get the right sort of body kit for the Suzuki in the UK. But Swifts are really big down under, so we had the body kit shipped all the way from Australia. It's a mean Japanese street-racer kit that completely changes the shape of the Swift. **martin**

# Interior

- 2 × Cobra Lemans recliner seats
- Camcorder JVC GZ-MG50
- Severed hand supplied by Silly Jokes
- Handprints supplied by Articole Studios
- Steering wheel re-trimmed in red leather
- Gearknob and handbrake handle re-trimmed in red leather supplied by Simoni Racing
- Pedal set (Rally Ergal)
- Grooming kit contains: Nose trimmer, all-in-one electric groomer, lip balm, moisturiser and aftershave

## Paint

- Paint: Jet Black Direct Gloss 4Q with CD Seal Primer supplied by House of Kolor
- Vinyl graphics supplied by Premier Signs
- Black Caliper Paint provided by Foliatec

❝ We built a case into the roof to house a film projector. Then we fitted new hinges to the bonnet so it flips up the 'wrong' way round: from the front of the car. And then I mounted a projector screen on the inside to complete the movie experience. We also fitted a mini digital camera in the dash and a screen to watch it back, so Jamie could practise his acting. Jamie is the first person in the UK to have the head unit we put in: not only does it play CDs, DVDs, MP3s, but will also store them onto its own hard drive: it's the daddy of all consoles... ❞ **bluey**

❝ Jamie's a fan of all things Japanese, so after we'd sprayed the Swift black, we went Manga mad: think Lucy Liu in Kill Bill. Plus we put Jamie's name into the graphics as well. ❞ **ronnie**

# Ice

- NEC projector, NEC-LT-710 provided by Just Projectors
- Stereo head units AVIC-HD1BT and DEH-30MP for sound effects by Pioneer
- 2 × subwoofers TS-SW124D, 2 pairs of TSA-1711 speakers and 2 pairs of TSA-1311 speakers by Pioneer
- 2 × 4 Channel Amps PRS-A700 provided by Pioneer
- 1 × 15in Blaupunkt roof-mounted screen

> " Jamie's wheels were a real horror story, real B-movie material. But I sorted him out with some 17-inch wheels: heat-treated alloys in platinum silver, black polished rim, with a low-profile tyre. " **junior**

# Wheels

- 17in rocket 4 alloy wheels supplied by TSW
- Yokohama 205/40/17 all round

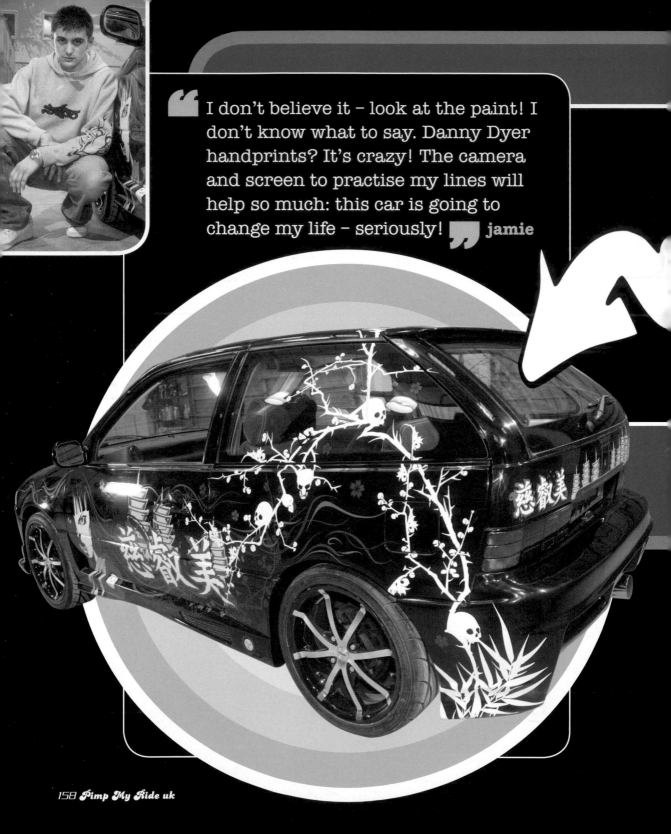

"I don't believe it – look at the paint! I don't know what to say. Danny Dyer handprints? It's crazy! The camera and screen to practise my lines will help so much: this car is going to change my life – seriously!" jamie

# Suzuki Swift
## Pimped

"It's the ultimate maxed-out ride – it's crazy." **westwood**

# Pimp's MC

**What cars from the show stood out for you?**

The Panda was a lot of fun – I liked the dude. The truth is I love all the pimpees. I feel they all really deserve it. That's the highlight of the show – when I'm at the doorstep and you see the surprise and the excitement. And at the end of the show, when you give the car back and it's wilder than their dreams could imagine, that's beautiful too. So I get to do the best parts of the show, without the hard work.

**Have you had any fantasy pimping on your own cars?**

No, my style's just standard big dawg stuff.

**Are you always doing stuff to your cars?**

Right now my car is with Ronnie, getting some paintwork done and some minor improvements. As soon as the series is over, the Street Team van will get a total rehaul. We got a lot of new ideas. We do about 100,000 miles a year in it.

**Do you get a 'friends and family' rate from the guys at the garage?**

I'm told I do. But I don't get other quotes. [laughs]

**After Pimp, can we expect to see more Westwood on TV?**

Yeah more Pimp My Ride UK. It's a beautiful thing this car game!

**As a big modification fan, have you learned anything from working with the garage more closely?**

Yeah, one of the things I've really learned a lot about is paint: Ronnie's taught me a lot about Kandy & Pearl – you can really win in this car game with paint.

**Do you get more attention when you're out, after being on Pimp?**

Yeah: it's love and I embrace that. A lot of young people embrace me, kids not old enough to listen to me on the radio or to

Can you do pimping yourself?
No - I'm a straight garage guy. I failed
all my woodwork and metalwork and
motor mechanics exams at school. I was
absolutely useless at that. So I struggle. I'm
definitely a guy with neat hands.

What do you do if your car breaks down?
Phone the AA.

You never tinker?
No – I'm not a car botherer. I like the
creative ideas – but I haven't self-pimped
since I was a teenager.

buy the Westwood albums. A lot of the 12-
and13-year-olds love Pimp My Ride UK,
they know me from that. A lot of time I'm
on the street and parents will come up and
say their kids love the show. It's a beautiful
thing. It's been very big out there.

VW
Beetle

# Please MTV, Pimp My Ride

**Pimpee...** *Sheerin Khosrowshahi*

Film student Sheerin calls her VW Beetle "Chloe". Her friends call it "the buggy of death". The Beetle is nearly 40 years old, but the way Sheerin drives, it'll be lucky to get there. It's dented at the side, concertinaed at the back and rusty all over. There are holes. Every panel tells a story. A horror story. Sheerin has shunts for fun.

When Chloe isn't crashing into other road users or stationary objects, she's breaking down. Every time Sheerin's driven home from university, she's ended up on the hard shoulder. But she loves her car. It may be scruffy – with just an ugly bit of gaffa tape where the radio used to be before it got nicked – but it's definitely loved.

Sheerin's been into Beetles since she was a little girl: her grandad drove one back in Iran, where the family's from. He used to show her pictures of it and she thought it was the coolest car in the world. Her mum knows the real score, though. She remembers the day Sheerin came home with the Bug. "The car looked like a piece of purple garbage."

Sheerin's ride has some nice touches: she loves her cow-print seat covers, for one. But the running repairs are just too expensive. Something's got to give. "She's like a friend to me," she says of the Beetle. "But if I don't get my car pimped, I'll have to get rid of it: I can't afford it anymore. This is Chloe's last chance."

## pimp dossier ...

» **Name:** Sheerin Khosrowshahi
» **Ride:** 1969 VW Beetle
» **Lives:** Sheffield
» **Daytime:** film student
» **Sounds:** punk rock, ska
» **Character:** fun, bubbly, bright
» **Dream job:** film editor. (Her favourite film director is Tim Burton)

» **Her friend Holly says...** "She's really blonde inside: a bit dizzy and ditzy."

## Westwood's verdict

Whoooooaaaaaaaaa! This car is rubbish – and if Westwood says this car is rubbish, don't take it with a pinch of salt – take it to the bank. It's a battered, beaten, bust, Beetle – it's crushed. Look at the bodywork: there's been heavy hit after heavy hit after heavy hit – it's like counting down the chart! She's been using the whole car as a bumper! What exactly is she saying with this ride? It's a mess!

> **"** She's got gaffa tape on the window; in fact she's got gaffa tape everywhere. Her gaffa game is strong. **"**
> **westwood**

# Pimp Plan...

" Bug? This thing looks like it's been swatted a million times, but by the time we're done with her, Sheerin's going to be the proud owner of one of the funkiest Beetles in town. The Beetle is an absolute classic – but this one is an embarrassment. This old girl needs some serious help. " **jamie**

" How can Sheerin practise her driving without actually going onto the road? I've come up with a way. She's going to have her very own track for racing Beetles – under her bonnet! I'm going to lay a track under her bonnet so she can practise her driving on some custom-made mini racing cars... " **jamie**

" Sheerin's a girl with a big, bold, beautiful personality and she needs a colour to reflect that. So I'm going for a shocking pink – and that's not all. We're going to pick up on that cow-print seat covering she loves – and milk it: we're going to put cowprint vinyl on the roof! " **ronnie**

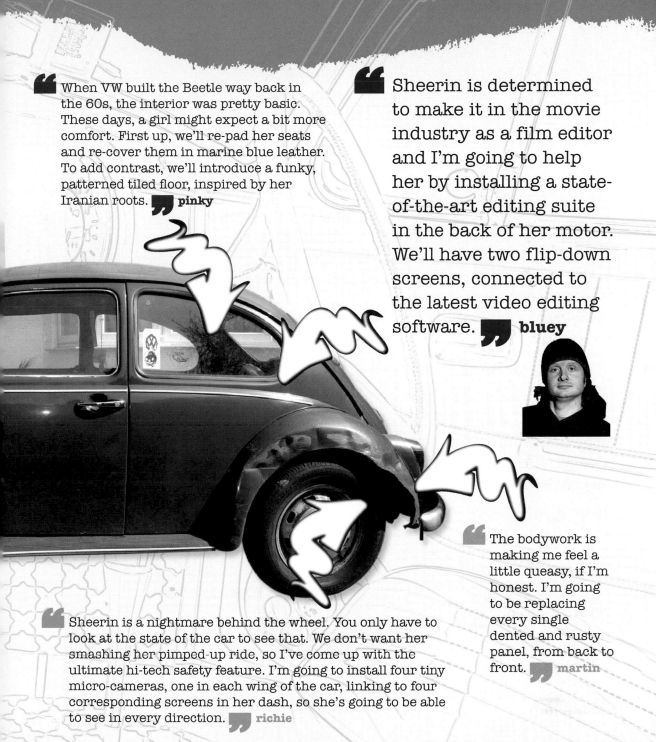

When VW built the Beetle way back in the 60s, the interior was pretty basic. These days, a girl might expect a bit more comfort. First up, we'll re-pad her seats and re-cover them in marine blue leather. To add contrast, we'll introduce a funky, patterned tiled floor, inspired by her Iranian roots. **pinky**

Sheerin is determined to make it in the movie industry as a film editor and I'm going to help her by installing a state-of-the-art editing suite in the back of her motor. We'll have two flip-down screens, connected to the latest video editing software. **bluey**

The bodywork is making me feel a little queasy, if I'm honest. I'm going to be replacing every single dented and rusty panel, from back to front. **martin**

Sheerin is a nightmare behind the wheel. You only have to look at the state of the car to see that. We don't want her smashing her pimped-up ride, so I've come up with the ultimate hi-tech safety feature. I'm going to install four tiny micro-cameras, one in each wing of the car, linking to four corresponding screens in her dash, so she's going to be able to see in every direction. **richie**

# Pimping It

The hardest part of pimping the Beetle was definitely the bodywork. It was in such a bad state. We ordered 23 different body panels – bonnet, wings, door handles, badges, everything – to get it sorted: it took Steve three days of extensive welding before we could even start pimping.

## Exterior

- Re-sprayed in specially mixed one-off Pink with Ice Blue Pearl from House Of Kolor
- Roof of car painted white from House Of Kolor
- Cow-print graphics added by Premier signs
- All damaged body panels replaced with thanks to Cool Air VW
- Pink underbody LED kit Varad ULS 410 supplied by Drivecast

"This car was rotten to the core. Before we could start on the process of making it look great, we had to make sure the chassis and the body shell were solid. After we had reinforced the chassis, making it stronger, the only possible course of treatment for the bodywork was a full transplant: we pulled off all the old panels and started again. There wasn't one single body panel on the car that Sheerin hadn't battered and bruised – but we've made it completely smooth as new." martin

# Interior

> Sheerin is really proud of her Iranian roots, so we reflected that by using Persian-style pieces of mosaic to create a fully tiled floor – inside the car! **jamie**

- Yarwood leather in Kensington Siren Blue with white piping covering the original seating

- For the first time ever – a car with a tiled floor! Authentic Persian tiles from Dar Interiors

- Crystal gear knob from Swarovski Crystal

- One-off Scalextric track built into bonnet space

- Picnic set from Sunshine Bits – complete with plates, cutlery, linen napkins, wine cooler and rug!

- Hand painted original Beetle racing cars

## Paint

"Sheerin's Beetle was really showing its age with its washed-out paint job – the purple had to go. We gave her a Bubblegum-Pink re-spray, leaving the roof plain white, so we could stick on a cowprint vinyl." ronnie

- Bremen MP74 Radio, CD, MP3 head unit supplied by Blaupunkt

- 4 × 6.5in-wide screen Blaupunkt IVMS 6502 monitors to four custom-fitted bullet parking cameras from Park It Right

- Bumper-mounted parking sensors front and rear from Park It Right

- 2 × amplifiers 1 × THA 480 and 1 × THA 280 from Blaupunkt

- Speakers – 8 × Blaupunkt mids & 8 Blaupunkt tweeters

# Ice

" We put in a really powerful laptop, manufactured by Rock and loaded with the latest editing software. It's connected to two 15-inch monitors installed in the roof: they fold down so you can view them from the back seat. Now Sheerin will have all the equipment she needs to make movies – wherever she is. We also installed a top-of-the-range head unit with 16 speakers for playing CDs and DVDs. " **bluey**

" The 15-inch rims we fitted are especially made for VWs and together with a low-profile tyre, they're going to help keep Sheerin on the straight and narrow. " **junior**

# Wheels

- 5.5 × 15in Prolines from Wolfrace Wheels
- Yokohama 185/65/15 all round.

> **"** Never in a million years did I think my car would get pimped. It's beautiful. I'm on top of the world; I just want to shout and scream my heart out. It's everything I ever wanted. **"** **sheerin**

# VW Beetle Pimped

> The guys at the garage have done it up big. Now Sheerin's Vee-dub is the baddest bug in Britain. **westwood**

# The Pimp Lowdown

# Technical Specifications

## Morris Minor

### Suspension
● Lowered suspension

### Wheels and Tyres
● 7.5 × 18in Matrix from Wolfrace with Toyo Proxes 215/35/18 tyres all round

### Exterior
● Re-sprayed in Tangerine Kandy from House of Kolor
● Bumpers, trims and wing-mirrors replaced
● Hot-rod stripe in yellow with silver border
● Smaller stripe around front emblem
● Replacement rear silencer with chrome outlet
● Retro roof rack
● Custom tailpipe

### Interior
● Re-sprayed dash as per exterior
● Magnolia leather from Andrew Muirhead & Son throughout
● Left dash compartment with fabricated, leather-trimmed enclosure for on-board printer lit up by 9in red Fuel neons
● Right-hand compartment with fabricated, leather-trimmed panel housing LED display counter
● Front and rear door panels re-fabricated and leather-trimmed with angular, retro-style speaker builds housing Pioneer TS-C1700R component mid/tweeter speakers
● Replacement front and rear seat; Cobra Le Mans, trimmed leather with contrasting orange top-stitch
● Headrests with orange-embroidered logos – 'Mrs' on driver seat and 'Mr' on passenger
● Rear of headrest fitted with Pioneer AVD-W62000 wide-screen monitors
● Sony PS2 and PS2-inverter mounted under driver seat in enclosure
● Pioneer CDX-P670 6-disc CD changer under passenger seat
● Replacement headlining with orange neoprene
● Fabricated centre console with retro-style Pioneer DEH-P77MP head unit
● Switching panel to operate new components
● Photo-storage compartment
● Re-trimmed leather Simoni Racing steering wheel X2350LYX
● Chrome gearknob 532200, handbrake lever FX7111GR, chrome pedal set 880PX all Simoni Racing from Auto Inparts
● Centre console contains Manfrotto Monopod 680 for digital camera and continues into rear with fabricated enclosure for Apple 12in iBook

### Boot
● Fabricated/leather-trimmed enclosures to the left- and right-hand side with 10in Subwoofer lit up by 9in red Fuel neons
● Rear enclosure with 2 × Pioneer amplifiers behind Perspex windows to power audio system
● Storage compartment with central division trimmed in neoprene

- Sit-down area in front of storage compartments trimmed in neoprene with 2 × leather foam cushions embroidered with 'Mrs' and 'Mr'
- Trim cover for inside boot lid with secure stay

## Ice
- 2-way Pioneer TS-C1700R component speakers in all door panels
- 2 × Pioneer AVD-W62000 wide-screen monitors fitted in the headrests
- Pioneer DEH-P77MP head unit
- 2 × 10in Pioneer subwoofers TS-SW124D mounted in the boot with 2 × PRS-X340 amplifiers
- Pioneer CDX-P670 6-disc CD changer

## Security
- Clifford Intellistart alarm with water jet warning squirters

## Pimp Extras:
- Apple 12in iBook with D-Link Bluetooth adaptor DBT-120
- Canon compact CP-330 printer
- 7.2 mega pixel Powershot S70 Canon camera with waterproof case
- Orange Nokia 6630 mobile phone with Bluetooth
- 2 x 'Pimped' Quiksilver surfboards and matching wetsuits
- Coga PA multi-sound horn to play the 'Wedding March'

*Golf Mark II*

## Suspension
- Koni suspension lowering kit

## Wheels and Tyres
- 7.5 × 18in Cataluyna Chrome from TSW with Yokohama 215/35/18 tyres all round

## Exterior
- Re-sprayed in Metallic Black from House of Kolor with red-sparkle flakes
- Big bumper kit added
- Lexus lights to rear
- DTM-style wing-mirrors
- Striped graphics across the bonnet
- Football shirt-style graphic on roof spelling "ASIF 3" in vinyl
- Replacement rear stainless steel silencer with DTM back box
- LSD door conversion kit
- Smoke-tinted windows
- Customised boot-cleaner concealed under back bumper

## Interior
- Red leather from Yarwood throughout
- Left dash compartment with fabricated, leather-trimmed enclosure for Sony PS2 and PS2-inverter
- Front and rear door panels re-fabricated and leather-trimmed with angular, retro-style speaker builds housing Pioneer TS-C1700R component mid/tweeter speakers
- Replacement front seats; Recaro Ergomeds, trimmed leather
- Remote-controlled, 8-point heated massage pads built into front seats
- Rear of headrest fitted with Audiobahn 6.5in screen monitors
- Replacement red headlining, sun-visors re-trimmed
- Fabricated centre console with Pioneer head unit X1
- Fabricated enclosures to left and right of back seats housing mini-fridges
- Switching panel to operate new components
- Re-trimmed leather Arcadia Simoni Racing steering wheel AR350/LR
- Elipse chrome gearknob 5922LR, handbrake lever F5S/LR, chrome pedal set 860PRX and chrome gear frame BX18 all Simoni Racing from Auto Inparts

## Boot
- Fabricated, leather-trimmed enclosures to the left- and right-hand side with face-mounted 10in subwoofers
- Rear enclosure with 2 × Audiobahn amplifiers to power audio system
- 12in linear actuator, raising the mount for flip-up 15.2in screen
- Pull-out tactics board, complete with pens and magnetic markers
- Storage compartment with central division for footballs etc.

## Ice

- Pioneer head unit X1
- 15.2in flip-up (we spun the flip down!) Centurion RE-1569 screen
- 2 × Centurion FD6569 6.5in screen monitors fitted in the headrests
- Component speaker sets ACIS63 from Audiobahn
- 2 × 10in subwoofers AW1000N and 2 × A1504DP amplifiers, both from Audiobahn, mounted in the boot
- AVSW4Q audio/video selector

## Security

- Viper alarm with mobile text alert system

## Pimp Extras

- Canon DV-MVX30i video camera with Jessops mini-tripod
- Red Sharp GXi Vodafone mobile
- Halfords mini tool kit
- Footballs, football boots, training bibs, nets, markers
- Football shirt signed by Thierry Henry

### Ford Granada Hearse

## Wheels and Tyres

- 7.5 × 18in blades from Wolfrace
- Toyo Proxes 225/45/18 tyres all round

## Exterior

- Re-sprayed in Brilliant White from House of Kolor
- Masked flames with red, orange and yellow fade blended by Airstream
- New white vinyl roof
- Blacked-out windows
- Chrome front and rear Nova 1967 bumpers
- Custom-made back box and exhaust TP32
- Rear lights painted white to blend with bodywork

- Custom-made chrome-embezzled quad front lights

## Interior

- Purple polka, wine- and black-coloured leather from Andrew Muirhead & Son throughout
- Rear seats trimmed in plum snakeskin vinyl
- Front-door panels re-fabricated, leather-trimmed with angular speaker builds housing 2-way component mid/tweeter speakers from JL Audio
- Front seats re-trimmed in black leather
- Cinema area with 2 × rear seats, in Scotia deluxe from Scot Seats, facing a Sony VPL-ES2 data projector screen with DVD player
- 3-way component set housed either side of screen
- Exclusive UV neons from Fuel lighting storage area under screen
- Replacement black leather headlining complete with 'Rock Hall of Fame' lit by red neons
- Re-trimmed centre console with Blaupunkt Bremen MP74 head unit
- Enclosure created behind the cinema seats with 2 × 12in subwoofers
- Simoni Racing X5350PUN-P steering wheel from Auto Inparts
- New black carpet laid throughout

## Boot

- Fabricated, leather-trimmed enclosures to left- and right-hand side with 2 Funktion One R1's
- Rear enclosure with E25 amplifier from MC$^2$
- Yamaha mixing console MG8/2FX to create outdoor concerts
- Storage compartment for band's equipment; fabricated symbol compartment to the floor
- Storage to left and right of mixing console

## Ice

- Blaupunkt Bremen MP74 Head units × 2 (front and centre)
- Blaupunkt DVD-ME2 player
- E25 amplifier mounted in the boot
- Also in the boot 2 × Resolution 1 speakers from Funktion One
- 2 × 12in JL Audio subwoofers J12 W4 mounted behind the cinema seats
- JL500/1 mono amp and JL300/4 amp from JL Audio
- 2-way component system enclosed in front-door cards CR635CSI
- JL Audio 3 way component set XR653CS (all JL Audio supplied by BBG Distribution)

## Security

- Clifford 650 alarm with Intellistart

## Pimp Extras
- Thunder and Lighting series microphone stand & boom with MXI2001 microphone from Yamaha
- Epiphone guitar from Gibson guitar
- Silver skull gearknob from Argoth
- Electric curtains from polesdirect.com
- Torpedo backlights from gokatgo.com
- Skeleton keyring from Hauntedshop
- Tim Westwood still from Peter Ashworth
- Rock stills from rockarchive.com

Fiat Panda

## Suspension
- Pi lowering suspension kit (made for a Panda!!!)

## Wheels and Tyres
- 7.5 × 17in Bushidos from Wolfrace
- Toyo Proxes 215/40/17 tyres all round

## Exterior
- Re-sprayed in metallic Lime-Gold Kandy from House of Kolor
- Camouflage-style graphics by Image Worx laid over the back third
- Exclusive custom-made GT5R Carisma Automotive kit
- Smoke-tinted windows from Nationwide Tints
- Custom-made trailer with fold-out skate ramps and grind pole produced by Wesbroom Engineering Ltd.

## Interior
- Nutmeg-coloured leather from Andrew Muirhead & Son throughout
- Wear-patches trimmed in Culverhouse & Sons black carbon-fibre-effect leather
- 3 × Cobra Misanos (2 in front and single seat in rear)

- GPS system NVE-N099P from Alpine with TME-M770 screen, housed in passenger's sun visor
- Alpine 9847 head unit
- Fabricated centre console with Ectaco TL-4 voice-activated language translator
- Switching panel to operate new components
- Flip-down 10.4in Audiobahn AVM104IRV screen for reclining single seat in back
- Fabricated roof cases, holding 2 × Enjoi skateboards, either side of rear seat lit by green neons
- 6 × 6.5 2-way Fusion component speakers housed (3 either side) above rear seat
- Fabricated armrests in the back seat housing an Xbox on one side and Alpine 6-CD changer CHA-S634 on the other
- Re-trimmed leather Bolide Simoni Racing steering wheel BO350/LR with chrome hub kit
- Touring chrome gearknob 522010/I, handbrake lever FX7111, chrome pedal set 890/X all Simoni Racing from Auto Inparts
- New carpet throughout

## Boot
- Fabricated, leather-trimmed half-pipe-style enclosures for 3 Fusion FE-402 amps lit with green neons
- 2 × 10in FEW-10 subwoofers mounted either side of half-pipe
- Floodlight on tailgate (for night-time skating)

## Ice
- Alpine 9847 head unit
- 6-disc CD changer CHA-S634 from Alpine
- GPS system NVE-N099P from Alpine with screen TME-M770
- 3 × 6.5 2-way Fusion component speakers in roof
- 2 × 10in Fusion subwoofers FEW-10
- FE-402 Fusion amps × 3 with amp wiring kit K-AK4
- Flip-down 10.4in Audiobahn AVM104IRV screen

## Security
- Clifford 650 alarm with Intellistart

**Ford Capri**

## Wheels and Tyres
- 7.5 × 17in chrome Hybrid from Wolfrace
- Toyo Proxes 205/40/17 tyres all round

## Exterior
- Re-sprayed with Cobalt-Blue Kandy over a silver base, both from House of Kolor
- Front and rear Mk5 Escort Cosworth bumpers customised to fit from Pro Sport
- New standard lights with extra fog lights on the front bumper
- RS2000 Ford Escort side skirts from Pro Sport
- Custom-extended bonnet power bulge
- Webasto Deluxe 300 soft-touch electric sunroof with rain sensor closing
- 3in custom-made, stainless steel trim, outward roll exhaust from Exhausts UK

## Interior
- White leather from Yarwood throughout, including headlining with blue piping on the seats
- 'S' logo embroidered onto top of seats and basketball court design on base and top of seats
- Black carpet trimmed with white-leather edging throughout
- Front door panels re-fabricated, leather-trimmed with angular speaker builds housing 2-way co-axial speakers from MTX Audio
- OQO Model 01 Ultra personal computer housed in front centre console, with flip-over mouse mat and Logitech V500 wireless mouse
- Custom-made 100% crystal 'pimp stick' gearknob with engraved 'S' logo by Swarovski
- 2 × front dials and speaker builds in the door cards surrounded by Swarovski crystals
- Simoni Racing handbrake lever F5S/LR from Auto Inparts
- Chrome and white-leather-trimmed steering wheel from Issotta
- Custom spinning storage area in centre of back with 'S' logo made from 500 Swarovski crystals lit by blue Fuel neons. Storage area contains shirts, ties and cufflinks from Thomas Pink on one side, and basketball clothing from AND1 UK on other.
- Clear Xbox housed behind driver's seat with controls extended to reach screen in boot
- Electric basketball scoreboard from Sportserve hidden in custom interior build between front seats and boot, which raises up via alarm remote, powered by linear actuators from Select products.
- Control panel for the scoreboard is housed behind passenger seat.
- 2 × MTX Audio component speakers either side of raising scoreboard
- Wilson basketball below each speaker
- Electric windows and central locking fitted

## Boot
- 2 × 12in subwoofers pushing out 1200 watts each
- 17in framed Sony LCD screen for Xbox
- Floating MTX amps either side of screen, lit underneath by blue neons
- Streetwires combo pod on display with wires disappearing into floor of boot build
- Matching white leather trim

## Ice
- FHL-17 Sony 17in LCD screen
- Exclusive Pioneer DEH-P70BT Bluetooth head unit, working in conjunction with Sony Ericsson K700i mobile phone from Orange
- Sledge Hammer MTX Audio dual Thunder 5500 12in subwoofers
- Thunder 3404 – 4 channel amp and Thunder 3401 – class D mono-black amp from MTX audio supplied by BBG distribution
- StreetWires cabling, fusing and accessories throughout

## Security
- Clifford 650 alarm with Intellistart and total closure

## Black Cab

### Wheels and Tyres
● Front: 16in chrome hubcaps with Toyo Proxes 195/50/16 tyres
● Back: 7.5 × 18in chrome matrix from Wolfrace with Toyo Proxes 225/35/18 tyres

### Exterior
● Re-sprayed in Purple Haze Pearl from House of Kolor
● Claret, snakeskin-textured vinyl roof with custom-matching front and rear snakeskin bumpers
● Blacked-out windows to side and rear
● New headlights with chrome surround
● Wing-mounted chrome round mirrors
● Custom made, Rolls-Royce-style grill with mini-camera mounted into top – image is viewed on screen in back of the taxi
● Boot decorated with cover art from Freaky Dancin' by the Happy Mondays
● Taxi-hire light which reads 'PIMP' with red background

### Interior (Front)
● Driver seat trimmed in black and red leather
● Passenger side door card with mammoth speaker build comprising 6 × Blaupunkt 6 × 9 speakers shaping an arrow pointing to VIP section.
● 12in Linear actuator pushing out passenger seat from under dash build trimmed in red leather and facing into the back
● Flip-down board with wide screen laptop with Traktor software and Numark mixer for the 'in-house' taxi DJ
● 4 × floor-mounted door entry white lights
● Black carpet laid throughout with red leather-trim around the edge

### Interior (Back)
● Curved couch in quilt-effect red leather and Lycra from Yarwoods with black padded edging
● Blaupunkt 6 × 9 speakers mounted at base of couch
● 14 × 6.5 screens mounted on roof surrounded by mirror tiles
● Leopard-print fabric roof lining
● 42in Sony plasma screen housed in red leather-trimmed frame
● Xbox clear housed under plasma
● 3 × 12in and 3 × 10in subwoofers on the back wall mounted in red leather and leopard print frames
● 4 × Laser crabs and 2 × strobes hidden in the back wall for nightclub effect
● Controls with 16 × switches
● 1 × head unit and 2 × DVD players from Blaupunkt
● 3 × StreetWires combo blocks and 2 × Power stations on display (a very small percentage of the mass of cabling hidden)
● Red and green neons from Fuel

### Boot
● Smoke machine which pumps into VIP section
● 8 × amps (4 × 1300w & 4 × 600w)
● 2 × optima yellow-top batteries from Autoleads
● 7 × standard 3-pin plug sockets – 3 of them remote-controlled!!

### Ice
● 4 × Blaupunkt TSA 1300 amps and 4 × TSA 460
● Woodstock DAB54 Blaupunkt digital radio/CD/MP3 player
● 13 × TSx693 3 way triaxial system 210w Blaupunkt speakers with back lighting kits
● 14 × IVMS-6502 6.5in colour TFT-LCD Blaupunkt monitors
● 3 × Blaupunkt TSw300 transparent high power speakers 600w single voice coil 12in subwoofers
● 3 × Blaupunkt TSw250 transparent high power speakers 540w single voice coil 10in subwoofers
● Numark DXM01USB-240V 24 bit mixer

### Security
● Under-car strobes and smoke canisters activated by Clifford G5 alarm

### Pimp Extras
● Ice bucket and champagne flutes
● Wide-screen HP laptop installed with Traktor mixing software
● DJ PCMCIA Soundcard from Indigo DJ
● Digitax taxi meter with customised receipt
● Flashing 'PIMP' taxi light on roof activated by alarm

**Nissan Sunny**

## Wheels and Tyres
- 7.5 × 18in Drift from Wolfrace
- Toyo 205/40/17 tyres all round
- Custom-designed 'Jack' vinyl centre cap made by Premier Signs

## Exterior
- Main body re-sprayed in Lime Gold Kandy from House of Kolor.
- Executive stripe and fade in matt yellow by Bee Bee Refinishing Supplies
- Bodykit by Erebuni. Style number 313 DTM Volvo 850
- Ecosse twin fog-lights
- Twin 3.5in pipe back box from Exhausts UK
- Yellow window-tint by Tintman

## Interior
- New Recaro Orthopead seats in front
- Door panels and centre panels of seats covered in 'Waikiki'-print fabric from Barkcloth Hawaii
- 'Aztec Yellow' leather on seat surrounds by Andrew Muirhead & Son
- Sports steering wheel XR 330 LY, trimmed in leather, from Auto Inparts
- Electric sunroof by Webasto
- Rear of headrests fitted with 6.5in screen monitors by Sony
- Sun-visors and ceiling re-trimmed in sky-blue suede from Boynett
- Sat Nav installed into driver's sun-visor, Sony model NAV-U50
- Sand-coloured carpet from Culverhouse and Sons
- Sand-filled clear plastic foot wells from Project Plastics, lit with red LED bars from Vara-
- Central bank of switches to operate new car components

- Chrome gearknob and chrome pedal set 860PGX from Auto Inparts
- SAD-therapy light box LTSAD001 fitted into glove box, supplied by Allergy Matters
- Two custom-made clocks in dash. One on London time one Kingston, Jamaica time. Made by Myclock
- 4 × 6.5in 2-way co-axial speakers supplied by BBG Distribution and MTX Audio

## Boot
- Vestax Handi Trax portable turntable
- 3 × 15in MTX subwoofers supplied by BBG Distribution
- Custom-built sliding shelf unit holding turntable and storage for 7in reggae singles
- Boot interior spray-painted in beach graffiti by Pro 7 Graff
- Amplification from 3 × MTX Thunders 3202 and 1 × MTX Thunder 3404

## Ice
- 2 × 6.5in headrest screens, Sony XVM-F65WL
- XBox playing Bicycle Casino from Zoo Digital Publishing
- Wireless MEX-R5 CD head unit from Sony
- In-car bongos built into back armrest supplied by DJM Music.

## Security
- Clifford Arrow 5 full closure alarm from GAP Security

## Pimp Extras
- Massage table from Therapy 2000
- Palm Life Drive personal organiser supplied by Kaizo

**BMW 316**

## Suspension
- Lowered on springs supplied by Apex

## Wheels and Tyres

- 17in Dayton Radial Lace wheels supplied by Dayton Wire Wheels
- Toyo 205/40/17 tyres all round

## Exterior

- Blueberry Pearl paint (DP42 over BC26), base coat and lacquer supplied by House of Kolor
- Front bumper and side skirts supplied by Raid UK
- Rear bumper supplied by Rieger
- Custom-made exhaust supplied by Exhausts UK
- M3 wing-mirrors and baseplates supplied by Raid UK
- Angel Eye headlight conversion supplied by Quality BMW Online
- Chrome wheel arch trim supplied by Eurocar Parts
- Aerial supplied by GK Motor Factors
- Suicide Door Kit supplied by Showtime Automotive
- Chrome wipers supplied by Isotta
- Number plates supplied by Colchester Radiators

## Interior

- Walnut interior film on dash supplied by FDT Technics / Foliotek
- Walnut steering wheel and boss supplied by Raid UK
- Gearknob and leather handbrake lever and gator supplied by Raid UK
- Brown cream leather supplied by Yarwoods
- Brown thread supplied by Culverhouse and Sons
- Beige Lamonta fabric for seats supplied by Boynetts
- Parchment Bison Vinyl for the Roof Supplied by Boynetts
- White Dial Kit (400sg) supplied by Lockwoods International
- Seat buttons supplied by Franklins
- Brown carpet supplied by Munchner Autostaff
- Blue 12in LED bars (HLW15BL) for boot supplied by Drivecast
- 2 × wine coolers supplied by Drinkstuff.com
- 3 × lockers supplied by Simply Lockers

## Ice

- 1 × Ice Pac 2 computer supplied by Karputer
- 2 × 7in motorised screens supplied by Spot Technologies
- 15in (MR1542) LCD screen supplied by Blaupunkt
- 2 × 6.5in Audiobahn Speakers (ACIS62) and 2 × Audiobahn 10in (AW101T) supplied by Tech Distribution
- 1 × Audiobahn 2 Channel amp (A1502DP) and 1 × Audiobahn (A1004DP) 4 Channel amp supplied by Tech Distribution
- 1 × Audiobahn Sub (AW100T) supplied by Tech Distribution
- Colour bullet camera supplied by Automotive Styling
- Data sim card supplied by Orange

- Nintendo DS games console with Mariocart supplied by Nintendo
- Quickbooks accountancy program supplied by Intuit
- Streetwires cabling and accessories supplied by BBG Distribution.

## Security

- Clifford Arrow 5 security system and 3 × remote poppers supplied by GAP security

Volkswagen Camper

## Wheels and Tyres

- 15in EMPI Wheel – MP5 spoke polished supplied by Big Boys Toys
- Toyo 185/60/15 all round

## Exterior

- Lower half re-sprayed in Gold Kandy from House of Kolor, with top half painted cream supplied by Bee Bee Refinishing Supplies
- Front chrome US-style bumper supplied by Paintbox
- Chrome windscreen-wipers from Custom and Commercial
- Chrome wing-mirrors supplied by Custom and Commercial
- Rear chrome US-style bumper supplied by Coolair
- Chrome side-sill step supplied by Custom and Commercial
- Chrome side trim kit supplied by Creative Engineering
- Chrome VW badges for front and rear supplied by Coolair
- Family tree on rear-window vinyl produced by Premier Signs
- Roof supplied by Big Boys Toys
- Heart-shaped exhaust supplied by Exhausts UK
- Number plates supplied by Colchester Radiators

- Chrome aerial supplied by Karmann Konnection
- Front indicators supplied by Coolair
- Front headlights supplied by Coolair
- Pop-out window frames supplied by Karmann Konnection

## Interior
- Front dash painted in Gold from House of Kolor
- Sun-visors supplied by Custom and Commercial
- Pedal set supplied by Custom and Commercial
- Scat shifter set supplied by Coolair
- Seat belts supplied by Custom and Commercial
- Cab floor covered in purple carpet, supplied by Culverhouse and Sons
- Front bench seat re-trimmed in cream leather supplied by Yarwoods, bench seat supplied by Custom Made Furniture
- Cream front door panels, leather supplied by Yarwoods
- Long contemporary cabinet with lacquered paint finish
- Test tube water-feature – test tubes supplied by Scientific Glass Laboratories, water enclosure supplied by Project Plastics
- Pump supplied by The Sealife Centre
- Easel supplied by Testrite US
- Electrical control panel – switches supplied by Rapid Electronics
- Under-unit changeable lighting – Perspex supplied by Project Plastics, lights and controller supplied by Drivecast
- Side-opening doors to house 15in Blaupunkt screen and 2 × Pioneer (ts-e 1796) speakers in each
- Motorised lips rock-and-roll bed trimmed in red alcantara, and fabricated from an original bed supplied by Custom Made Furniture. Linear actuators supplied by Select Products
- Corner cabinet to house teasmaid from Russell Hobbs
- Panels between windows trimmed in cream leather, with cream curtains
- 2 × Webasto Hollandia 500 panoramic sunroofs
- Curtain rail supplied by J&S Upholstery
- Fibre-optic back wall by Optic Lighting
- Rear window tinted black, tint performed by Tintman

## Ice
- Pioneer head unit DEH-P6800MP
- 2 × 15in Blaupunkt screens in side doors
- 15in Blaupunkt screen in roof panel
- 2 × 17cm Pioneer (ts-e 1796) speakers in each door
- Pioneer XDVP 9 DVD player
- Vid sig amp 4-way supplied by Automotive Styling

## Security
- Clifford alarm supplied by GAP security system

## Pimp Extras
- NEC 343i Mobile Phone
- Weather Forecast Unit BA312E built into roof and supplied by Oregon Scientific

## Volkswagen Polo

## Wheels and Tyres
- 7 × 17in Chrome Jet X from Rimstock
- Toyo 205/40/17 tyres all round

## Exterior
- Main section of car painted in Brilliant White from House of Kolor with Silver on bottom section in classic aviation style
- Pimpee's 'flying colours' along side of car in Magenta and Passion from House of Kolor
- "L" and "LANA01" logos designed by Dan Sutherland at MTV and printed by Premier Signs
- Bodykit: supplied by PSG Bodystyling. New front grill (Reiger C00114077). Front bumper Reiger (C00109614). Rear bumper (Reiger C00109555). Side skirts (Reiger D00047004 & 005). GT5 roof spoiler
- Wheel arches widened with G60 arch kit to improve car profile
- New Angel Eyes front lights supplied by GBK Performance
- M3-style wing-mirrors with indicators from GBK Performance, with hand-made mirror baseplates
- Unique Twin 3.5in centre-exit exhaust hand-made by Magnex
- Back and rear side-windows tinted in smoked-Limousine-style by Tintman
- Door handles removed and bodywork smoothed to improve car aerodynamics. Doors open on pop-locks supplied by Gap Security

- Windscreen wipers simplified to single wiper. Conversion kit from Edworthy's Online
- Side skirt neon 'landing lights', VARAD SL 200 LED BARS supplied by Drivecast
- Sunroof repaired
- New aerial fitted

## Interior
- Four genuine Boeing 747 seats flown in from Southern Aviation Services, San Antonio, Texas, USA
- 'No Smoking' and 'Fasten Seatbelt' signs also supplied by Southern Aviation Services and fitted to custom-built central console of switches to operate car's new functions
- Seats padded for extra luxury and re-upholstered in a combination of raspberry- and wine-coloured leather by Andrew Muirhead & Son
- Chrome 'Universal Rally' pedal set, 'Winner' gearknob and new sports steering wheel X2 33 with Elegance Universal handbrake lever all from Auto Inparts, with tailor-made handbrake gator and steering wheel re-trimmed in grey and raspberry leather to match interior seats
- Ceiling re-trimmed in Lamonta Blush suede from Boynett
- Grey-coloured carpet for executive limo look

## Boot
- 1 × 4 (Fusion 504) channel amp from Fusion in white
- Housing for trolley, upholstered in suede and displaying Lana's flying logo
- VHS 'black box' recorder to record CCTV camera footage on to. Model DAEWOO SV872P

## Ice
- 4 × screens fitted to view DVDs and in-car CCTV footage
- Front visors fitted with 2 × Blaupunkt IVMS 6502
- Headrests fitted with 2 × Fusion 700 R
- DVD player SAV DVD built into glove box from Fusion
- Front loading CD head unit SCD 255 S from Fusion
- 4 × 17cm 2-way co-axial marine speaker in white FSM 65 – FPS 652

## Security
- Full alarm with pop-lock doors, central locking and remote Intellistart from GAP Security. Model; Concept 650 with 2 × pop-locks

## Pimp Extras
- Electronic mirror-ball from Electrovision fitted to ceiling. Illuminated by laser pod light supplied by Ben Rousseau.
- Bullet colour CCTV camera from Automotive Styling.
- Custom-built in-car service trolley fully loaded with snacks, drinks and Benefit cosmetics.

- Internal Coga PA system and musical horn supplied by Demon Bikes
- New Nokia N70 phone with Nokia 616 Bluetooth car kit for wireless hands-free conversations
- New luggage set from Antler. Model 'Smart' in pink
- Limited edition 'Pimp My Ride' sick-bags supplied by Flightstore
- Tartan lambswool blankets in 'Lindsey' tartan from Scotweb

Suzuki Swift GTi

## Wheels and Tyres
- 17in rocket 4 alloy wheels supplied by TSW
- Yokohama 205/40/17 tyres all round

## Exterior
- Paint: Jet Black Direct Gloss 4Q with CD Seal Primer supplied by House of Kolor
- Jetspeed Bodykit supplied by Evofusion
- White LED lights (SL200) for projector screen from Drivecast
- Japanese-style exhaust hand-crafted by Exhausts UK
- Bonnet rising 8in linear actuator supplied by Select
- Under-bonnet projector display provided by Carisma
- Japanese Manga-style graphics created by Engine Design
- Vinyl graphics supplied by Premier Signs
- Black Caliper paint provided by Foliatec

## Interior
- 2 × Cobra Lemans recliner seats and subframes by Cobra
- Camcorder JVC GZ-MG50 provided by JVC
- Severed hand supplied by Silly Jokes
- Spring mechanism for hand supplied by Earnest Does
- Handprints supplied by Articole Studios
- Steering wheel re-trimmed in red leather supplied by Auto Inparts

- Pedal set (Rally Ergal) provided by Auto Inpart
- Gearknob re-trimmed in red leather supplied by Simoni Racing
- Handbrake with hand-made red leather gator supplied by Simoni Racing
- LEDs for vanity mirror supplied by GK Motorfactors
- 5 × pairs of Red Varad 12in LED light bars (HLW15) for boot supplied by Drivecast
- Perspex for boot amp covers supplied by Project Plastics
- Grooming kit containing Wahl nose trimmer, Remmington all-in-one electric groomer and lip balm, moisturiser and aftershave provided by Nivea.
- Green, white and red leather supplied by Yarwoods
- Red carpet for floor supplied by Munchenhoff
- Switches provided by Carisma
- 500-watt power inverter supplied by Mastervolt UK

## Ice
- NEC projector NEC-LT-710 provided by Just Projectors
- Stereo Head Unit AVIC-HD1BT supplied by Pioneer
- Stereo Head Unit DEH-30MP for sound effects supplied by Pioneer
- 2 × subwoofers TS-SW124D supplied by Pioneer
- 2 pairs of TSA-1711 speakers supplied by Pioneer
- 2 pairs of TSA-1311 speakers supplied by Pioneer
- 2 × 4 Channel amps PRS-A700 provided by Pioneer
- 1 × 15in roof-mounted screen provided by Blaupunkt

## Security
- Clifford arrow 5 alarm with central locking and pop-lock supplied by GAP Security

## Pimp Extras
- Sumo suits supplied by I want one of those
- Nissan Skyline provided by CICarScene
- Mazda RX-7 provided by Jimmy's Mazda RX-7 Specialists

**Volkswagen Beetle**

## Wheels & Tyres
- 5.5 × 15in Proline's from Wolfrace Wheels Yokohama 185/65/15 tyres all round

## Exterior
- Re-sprayed in specially mixed one-off Pink with Ice Blue Pearl from House Of Kolor
- Roof painted White from House Of Kolor
- Cow-print graphics added by Premier Signs
- Replacement body panels with thanks to Coolair VW
- Replacement headlight bezels and rear bumper mounting brackets
- Chrome front and rear bumpers
- Passenger front glass – quarter glass
- Genuine VW aerial
- Chrome bonnet-handle and blades
- Horn grills
- T1 script badge
- Chrome tailpipes
- Chrome 'Volkswagen' badge from Cool Air
- Quarter rear panel
- 2 × new running boards
- 1 × new bonnet
- Front and rear wings – N/S and O/S
- Bonnet trim in chrome
- Locks for front doors and boot
- Rear lights
- Window lifter and rubber
- Pink underbody LED kit Varad ULS 410 from Drivecast

## Interior
- Yarwood leather in Kensington Siren Blue with white piping covering the original seating
- Authentic Persian tiles from Dar Interiors
- Crystal gearknob from Swarovski Crystal
- Ceiling trimmed in white vinyl

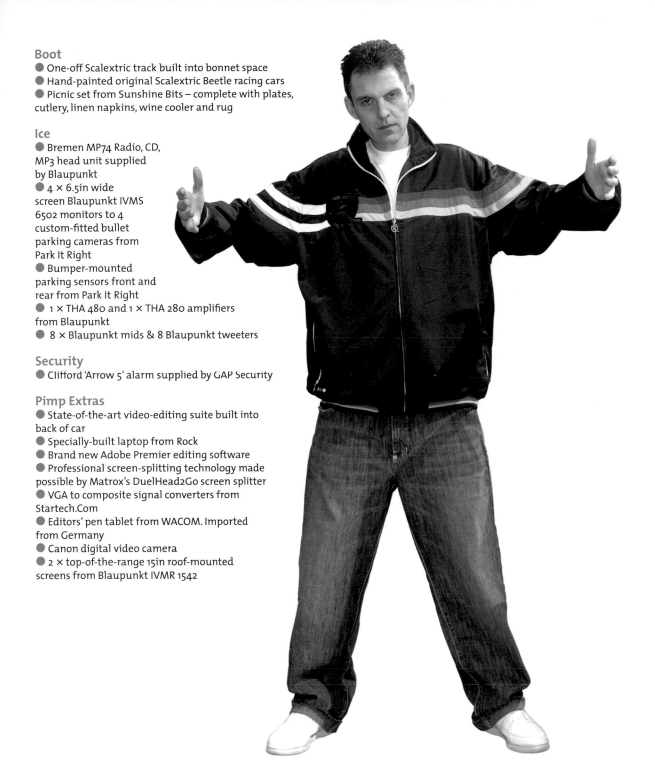

## Boot
● One-off Scalextric track built into bonnet space
● Hand-painted original Scalextric Beetle racing cars
● Picnic set from Sunshine Bits – complete with plates, cutlery, linen napkins, wine cooler and rug

## Ice
● Bremen MP74 Radio, CD, MP3 head unit supplied by Blaupunkt
● 4 × 6.5in wide screen Blaupunkt IVMS 6502 monitors to 4 custom-fitted bullet parking cameras from Park It Right
● Bumper-mounted parking sensors front and rear from Park It Right
● 1 × THA 480 and 1 × THA 280 amplifiers from Blaupunkt
● 8 × Blaupunkt mids & 8 Blaupunkt tweeters

## Security
● Clifford 'Arrow 5' alarm supplied by GAP Security

## Pimp Extras
● State-of-the-art video-editing suite built into back of car
● Specially-built laptop from Rock
● Brand new Adobe Premier editing software
● Professional screen-splitting technology made possible by Matrox's DuelHead2Go screen splitter
● VGA to composite signal converters from Startech.Com
● Editors' pen tablet from WACOM. Imported from Germany
● Canon digital video camera
● 2 × top-of-the-range 15in roof-mounted screens from Blaupunkt IVMR 1542

## A

Adobe: www.adobe.co.uk
Allergy Matters: www.allergymatters.com
Alpine: www.alpine.com
Apexwww.apex-suspension.co.uk
Anchorfast: www.reca-uk.com
AND 1: www.and1.co.uk
Andrew Muirhead & Son Ltd:
    www.muirhead.co.uk
Antler: www.antler.co.uk
Apple: www.apple.com/uk
Argoth: www.argoth.co.uk
Articole Studios: www.articolestudios.co.uk
Audiobahn: www.audiobahn.com
Auto Inparts: www.autoinparts.com
Autoleads: www.autoleads.co.uk
Automotive Styling: www.automotivestyling.co.uk

## B

Barkcloth Hawaii: www.barkclothhawaii.com
BaySixty6: www.baysixty6.com
BBG Distribution: www.bbg.eu.com
Bee Bee Refinishing Supplies: www.bee-bee.co.uk
Ben Rousseau: www.benrousseau.co.uk
Benefit: www.benefitcosmetics.co.uk
Big Boys Toys: www.bigboyztoys.co.uk
Blaupunkt: www.blaupunkt.com
Bloomsbury: www.tbp-autotrims.co.uk
Bosch: www.boschtools.com
Boynett: www.boynett.com
Bugjam: www.bugjam.co.uk

## C

Canon: www.canon.co.uk
Carisma: www.carismaautomotive.co.uk
Centurion: www.centurionsystems.co.uk
Clifford Alarm: www.cliffordalarm.co.uk
Cober Engineering: www.cober.co.uk
Cobra: www.cobraseats.com
Coga: www.cogapa.com
Colchester Radiators: Telephone: 01206 799559
Cool Air: www.coolairvw.co.uk
CPU Muscle Car Parts www.cpucarparts.com
Creative Engineering:
    www.creative-engineering.com
Culverhouse and Sons: Telephone:
    020 8858 9717
Custom and Commercial:
    www.customandcommercial.com
Custom Made Furniture: www.busfurniture.co.uk

## D

Dar Interiors: www.darinteriors.com
Dayton Wire Wheels: www.daytonwirewheels.com
Demon Bikes: www.demonbikes.com
Dewalt: www.dewalt.co.uk
Digitax: www.digitax-uk.com
DJ Store: www.djstore.co.uk
DJM Music: www.djmmusic.com
Drinkstufff: www.drinkstuff.com
Drivecast: www.drivecast.co.uk

## E

Ecosse: www.ecosse-peugeot.co.uk

Ectaco: www.ectaco.com
Edworthy's Online: www.edworthys.co.uk
Electrovision: www. www.electrovision.co.uk
EMPI Wheel: www.vw-online.co.uk
Engine: www.enginecreative.co.uk
Enjoi skateboards: www.enjoico.com
Erebuni: www.erubunicorp.com
Eurocar parts: www.eurocarparts.com
Exhausts UK: www.exhaustsuk.co.uk

FDT Technics / Foliotek: www.ftd-technics.de
Festool & Sata: www.minden-ind.co.uk
Flightstore: www.flightstore.co.uk
Franklins: www.franklinautoparts.com
Fuel lighting: www.liquidinjuredhearing.com
Funktion One: www.funktion-one.com
Fusion: www. fusioncaraudio.com

GAP Security: www.gapsecurity.co.uk
GBK Performance: gbkperformance.co.uk
Gibson guitar: www.gibson.com
GK Motor Factors: Telephone: 01376 500016
GoKatGo.com

Halfords: www.halfords.com
Hauntedshop: www.hauntedshop.co.uk
House of Kolor: www.houseofkolor.com

I Want One of Those: www.iwantoneofthose.com
Image Worx: www.image-worx.co.uk
Indasa Abrasnes: www.indasa.pt
Innotec: www.innotecworld.com
Indigo DJ: www.echoaudio.com
Inseat Solutions: www.relaxor.com
Intuit: www.quickbooks.co.uk
Isotta: www.isotta.com

J & S Upholstery: www.vwinteriors.com
Jazz Publishing: www.volkswagencamper.co.uk
Jetspeed: www.jetspeed.com.au
JL Audio: www.jlaudio.com
Just Projectors: www.projectors.co.uk
JVC: www.jvc.co.uk

Karmann Konnection:
      www.karmannkonnection.com
Karputer: www.karputer.co.uk
Koni Suspension: www.konisuspension.com

Lexus lights: www.extremeautoaccessories.co.uk
Lockwoods international: www.superdials.com

Magnex: www.magnexexhausts.com
Mastervolt: www.mastervolt.co.uk

Max Power: www.maxpower.co.uk
Meguiars www.meguiars.co.uk
MC2: www.mc2-audio.co.uk
Morris Minor Centre: www.morrisminor.co.uk
Myclock: www.myclock.co.uk
MTX Audio: www.mtxaudio.com

Nationwide Tints: Telephone: 01255 430070
NEC: www.necgroup.co.uk
New Deal Skates: www.nds.co.uk
Nintendo: www.nintendo-europe.com
Nivea: www.nivea.co.uk
Nokia: www.nokia.co.uk
Numark: www.numark.com

O2: www.o2.co.uk
Optic Lighting: www.opticlighting.co.uk
OQO www.oqo.com
Orange: www.orange.co.uk.
Oregon Scientific: www.oregonscientific.co.uk

Paintbox: www.thepaintbox.co.uk
Palm Life Drive: www.palm.com/uk
Park It Right: www.parkitright.com
Pi Suspension: www.p-i.co.uk
Pioneer: www.pioneer.co.uk
Poles Direct. www.polesdirect.com
Premier Signs: www.premier-signs.co.uk
Pro 7 Graff: www.pro7graff.com
Pro Sport: www.prosportuk.com

Project Plastics: www.projectplastics.co.uk
PSG Bodystyling: www.psgbodystyling.co.uk

Quality BMW Online: www.bmwworld.com
Quiksilver surfboards: www. www.quiksilver.com

Raid UK: www.raid-rdi.com
Rapid Electronics: www.rapidonline.com
Recaro Ergomeds: www.recaro.com
Remington: www.remington.co.uk
Rides Magazine: www.rides-mag.com
Rieger: www.tuning.co.uk/rieger
Rimstock wheels: www.rimstock.co.uk
Rock: www.rockdirect.com
Rockarchive.com
Russell Hobbs: www.russell-hobbs.com

SAAB: www.saab.co.uk
Samba: www.sambasports.co.uk
Scalextric: www.scalextric.com
Scientific Glass Laboratories:
www.scientificglass.co.uk
Scot Seats: www.scotseats.com
Scotweb: www.scotwebstore.com
Select Products: www.selectproducts.com
Sennheiser: www.sennheiser.co.uk
Showtime Automotive: www.autofashion.co.uk
Silly Jokes: www.sillyjokes.co.uk
Simoni Racing: www.simoniracing.com
Simply lockers: www.simplylockers.co.uk

Sony: www.sony.co.uk
Soundlab: www.soundlab.co.uk
Spalding: www.spalding.com
Sportserve: www.sportserve.co.uk.
Spot Tecnologies: www.spottechnologies.co.uk
Startech.Com: www.startech.com
StreetWires: www.streetwires.com
Sunshine Bits: www.sunshinebits.com
Swarovski: www.swarovski.com

Tao Sport: www.taosport.co.uk
Tartan Video www.tartanvideo.com
Tech Distribution: www. techdistributionltd.co.uk
Teng Tools: www.toolstars.co.uk
Testrite US: www.testrite.com
The Sealife Centre: www.sealifeeurope.com
Therapy 2000: www.therapy2000.com
Thimbles Fabrics www.thimblesfabrics.co.uk
Thomas Pink: www.thomaspink.co.uk
Tintman: www.tintman.co.uk
Tokyopop UK: www.tokyopop.com
Torque tools: www.torque-tools.co.uk
Toyo tyres: www.toyo.co.uk
Traktor: www.native-instruments.com
TSW wheels: www.tsw.com

Varad: www.varad.com
Vestax Handi Trax: www.vestax.co.uk
Viper alarm: www.caralarmuk.com
Vodafone: online.vodafone.co.uk
Volkswagen: www.volkswagen.co.uk

Volksworld: www.volksworld.com

Wacom: www.wacom-europe.com
Wahl: www.wahl.co.uk
Waterloo Industries: www.waterlooindustries.com
Webasto: www.webasto.com
Westbroom Engineering Ltd: Telephone:
     01206 576959
Wilson: www.wilson.com
Wolfrace wheels: www.woolfrace.net
Wow Automotive UK: Telephone: 0118 935 2838

Xbox: www.xbox.com

Yamaha: www.yamaha.co.uk
Yarwoods Leather: www.yarwood.co.uk.
Yokohama tyres: www.yokohamatire.com

Zoo Digital Publishing:
     www.zoodigitalpublishing.com

# Acknowledgements

## Acknowledgements
'Pimp My Ride UK' is based on the United States Series
'Pimp my Ride'
Created by Rick Hurvitz and Bruce Beresford-Redman

## Tim Westwood
Shout out to everyone who loves Pimp My Ride UK and the
creative car customisation game. And a special thanks to the
hardworking production team who make the show happen;
Howie, Sean, Tomek, Mat, Ann, Jules, Christina N, Stuart, Lucy,
Tom, Seema, Andrea, Dan S, Becs, Noel, Louise, Dan B, Chris H,
Kirsteen, Claire, Laura, Chris P, Christina I James and Lisa. And
the camera crew: Olly, Robbie, Ben, Jon. The guys at the garage
– Carisma: Jamie, Pinky, Ronnie, Bluey, Martin, Junior, Richie,
Steve, Matty. And my crew - Justice Entertainment: Maricel, Dre,
Alex, Brad, Amelie, Adam, Toni and Kerry.

## For MTV Networks Series Development USA
EXECUTIVE IN CHARGE OF PRODUCTION: Beth Greenwald

EXECUTIVE VP MTV SERIES ENTERTAINMENT: Lois Clark Curren

EXECUTIVE PRODUCERS: Rick Hurvitz, Bruce Beresford-Redman

## For MTV Networks UK & Ireland
EXECUTIVE PRODUCER: Sean Murphy

SERIES PRODUCER: Howie Jaffe

PRODUCER: Tomek Mikulin

DIRECTORS: Stuart Bamforth, Mat Hodgson, Christina Nutter,
Jules Watkins, Ann Wilson

PRODUCTION MANAGEMENT: James Breadin, Justine Roberts

PRODUCTION CO-ORDINATOR: Christina Isler

MARKETING MANAGER: Andrea Harris

PRESS and PR: Mandy Hershon, Eleanor Parker

ASSISTANT PRODUCERS: Noel Cowan, Lucy Davie, Rebecca Hall,
Andrea Madden, Louise Payne, Dan Van Den Bosch

RESEARCHERS: Tom Gent , Chris Hyndman , Seema Patel,
Kirsteen Rodger

RUNNERS: Claire Selim, Laura Somers

CAMERA: Olly Wiggins, Ben Spence

CAMERA ASSISTANT: Jon Kassell

DV OPERATORS: Chris Phillips, Dan Sully

SOUND: Robbie Campbell

EDITORS: Marcus Alcock, Chris Baker, Steve Brown, David Frisby,
Nick Scullard

DUBBING MIXER: Ian Marriott-Smith

MAKE-UP: Lisa Mejuto

Huge thanks to all the manufacturers and suppliers (you know
who you are) for their continued support and generosity.

Tim Westwood for making it BIG!

And last but not least; Jamie Shaw and the crew at Carisma
Automotive; Pinky, Ronnie, Bluey, Martin, Junior, Richie, Steve &
Matty, for turning those fantasy vehicles into reality.

## Picture credits
Before and after photography of cars © Doug Peters, 2006

Makeover photography for cars 1-6 © Karen Lauenborg, 2006
www.pinkcreative.co.uk

Makeover photography for cars 7-12 © Richie Don, 2006
www.djrichiedon.com

Marketing photos of Carisma team and Tim Westwood © Adam
Lawrence, 2006

## For Essential Works
TEXT: Duncan Steer

DESIGNERS: Kate Ward, Michael Duffy, Michael Gray

EDITORS: Annie Blinkhorn, Dipli Saikia